Institute of Leadership
& Management

superseries

Organizing and Delegating

FIFTH EDITION

Published for the
Institute of Leadership & Management

ELSEVIER

AMSTERDAM • BOSTON • HEIDELBERG • LONDON • NEW YORK • OXFORD
PARIS • SAN DIEGO • SAN FRANCISCO • SINGAPORE • SYDNEY • TOKYO
Pergamon Flexible Learning is an imprint of Elsevier

Pergamon
Flexible
Learning

716

Pergamon Flexible Learning is an imprint of Elsevier
Linacre House, Jordan Hill, Oxford OX2 8DP, UK
30 Corporate Drive, Suite 400, Burlington, MA 01803, USA

First edition 1986
Second edition 1991
Third edition 1997
Fourth edition 2003
Fifth edition 2007

Editor: David Pardey

Based on material in previous editions of this work

The views expressed in this work are those of the authors and do
not necessarily reflect those of the Institute of Leadership &
Management or of the publisher

Notice
No responsibility is assumed by the publisher for any injury and/or damage to persons or
property as a matter of products liability, negligence or otherwise, or from any use or operation
of any methods, products, instructions or ideas contained in the material herein

British Library Cataloguing in Publication Data
A catalogue record for this book is available from the British Library

Library of Congress Cataloguing in Publication Data
A catalogue record for this book is available from the Library of Congress

ISBN 978-0-08-046422-0

For information on all Pergamon Flexible Learning publications
visit our website at http://books.elsevier.com

Institute of Leadership & Management
Registered Office
1 Giltspur Street
London
EC1A 9DD
Telephone: 020 7294 2470
www.i-l-m.com
ILM is part of the City & Guilds Group

Typeset by Charon Tec Ltd (A Macmillan Company), Chennai, India
www.charontec.com
Printed and bound in Great Britain

07 08 09 10 11   10 9 8 7 6 5 4 3 2 1

Working together to grow
libraries in developing countries

www.elsevier.com | www.bookaid.org | www.sabre.org

ELSEVIER   BOOK AID International   Sabre Foundation

Contents

Series preface

Whether you are a tutor/trainer or studying management development to further your career, Super Series provides an exciting and flexible resource to help you to achieve your goals. The fifth edition is completely new and up-to-date, and has been structured to perfectly match the Institute of Leadership & Management (ILM)'s new unit-based qualifications for first line managers. It also harmonizes with the 2004 national occupational standards in management and leadership, providing an invaluable resource for S/NVQs at Level 3 in Management.

Super Series is equally valuable for anyone tutoring or studying any management programmes at this level, whether leading to a qualification or not. Individual workbooks also support short programmes, which may be recognized by ILM as Endorsed or Development Awards, or provide the ideal way to undertake CPD activities.

For learners, coping with all the pressures of today's world, Super Series offers you the flexibility to study at your own pace to fit around your professional and other commitments. You don't need a PC or to attend classes at a specific time – choose when and where to study to suit yourself! And you will always have the complete workbook as a quick reference just when you need it.

For tutors/trainers, Super Series provides an invaluable guide to what needs to be covered, and in what depth. It also allows learners who miss occasional sessions to 'catch up' by dipping into the series.

Super Series provides unrivalled support for all those involved in first line management and supervision.

Unit specification

Title:	Organizing and delegating		Unit Ref:	M3.14
Level:	3			
Credit value:	1			

Learning outcomes *The learner will*	Assessment criteria *The learner can (in an organization with which the learner is familiar)*	
1. Know how to organize people to achieve objectives	1.1	Explain the importance of making effective and efficient use of people's knowledge and skills while planning the team's work to achieve objectives
	1.2	Use *one* technique to schedule and allocate work to the team and individuals
	1.3	Explain how human resource planning can be used to assure output and quality
2. Know how to delegate to achieve workplace objectives	2.1	Give *one* example of delegation and *one* example of empowerment in the workplace
	2.2	Identify *one* barrier to delegation and *one* mechanism to support delegation
	2.3	Explain *one* technique that could be used to monitor the outcomes of delegation in the workplace
	2.4	Review the effectiveness of feedback, recognition and reward techniques in the workplace

Workbook introduction

1 ILM Super Series study links

This workbook addresses the issues of *Organizing and Delegating*. Should you wish to extend your study to other Super Series workbooks covering related or different subject areas, you will find a comprehensive list at the back of this book.

2 Links to ILM qualifications

This workbook relates to the learning outcomes of Unit M3.21 Organizing and delegating from the ILM Level 3 Award, Certificate and Diploma in First Line Management.

3 Links to S/NVQs in management

This workbook relates to the following Unit of the Management Standards which are used in S/NVQs in Management, as well as a range of other S/NVQs:

B6. Provide leadership in your area of responsibility
D6. Allocate and monitor the progress and quality of work in your area of responsibility

4 Workbook objectives

Delegation allows you to share some of your work and responsibilities with your team members, and it is an important skill for managing, organizing and developing your team.

In this workbook we will be exploring how you allocate work to your team, what delegation means, why it is important and what it involves. Then we will turn to the question of how to delegate successfully.

The workbook helps you to allocate work and put effective delegation into practice in your own work.

But what happens to the work in your team when you aren't there? Does the work still get done, or does it just stumble along until you get back? Many first line managers and team leaders report that there is usually a huge backlog of questions and problems waiting for them as soon as they walk through the door.

On one level this can be a great comfort – showing, as it does, just how important the manager is to the work of his or her section. But you probably agree that such dependence can put enormous pressures on any manager. It also suggests that the manager's team is not working together effectively, and perhaps that the manager is not developing the overall competence of the team. But one of the major responsibilities of managers is to build a team which can get the work done efficiently and effectively.

4.1 Objectives

When you have worked through this workbook you will **be better able to:**

- plan and allocate work to your team;
- explain why delegation is an important management technique;
- use the process of delegation to delegate effectively;
- control your workteam more efficiently.

5 Activity planner

The following Activities require some planning so you may want to look at these now.

Activity 25 asks you to draw up a work diary so you can get a clear idea of what you actually do during the day, rather than what you think or plan to spend your time doing.

Activities 27, 28, 29, 31, 33, 34, 35, 36, 37, 39 and 40 are a series of 11 Activities which guide you through the process of effective delegation.

Some or all of these Activities may provide the basis of evidence for your S/NVQ portfolio. All Portfolio Activities and the Work-based assignment are signposted with this icon.

The icon states the elements to which the Portfolio Activities and Work-based assignment relate.

Session A
Planning and allocating work

1 Introduction

The primary responsibility of first line managers is to make sure that the teams they manage do their work efficiently and effectively. Efficiently means that they use the minimum of resources to the maximum effect. Effectively means making the best use of the resources so that the goods or services that are produced are to the required quality standards. Everything you do is about achieving that goal.

To do this you need to ensure that the people you manage, the people in the team you lead, are making the best use of their skills to do the tasks that are required, what has sometimes been described as 'working smarter not harder'. In this first session we will explore how you can make sure that you are doing this, identifying the tasks that need doing, the people you have available to do them, and how best to match the one to the other.

2 What needs to be done?

Most organizations have some system for planning their future workload. The level of detail and the length of time over which this planning extends depends on the type of organization and its market. For example, an oil refinery engaged in continuous production, 24 hours a day, seven days a week, 52 weeks a year, may well have plans for the production of different categories of fuel (diesel, petrol, heating oil, etc.) throughout the year. On the other hand, a hairdresser can only plan a week or so ahead, based on customer bookings. An oil refinery cannot switch production off and on at will, whereas a hairdresser can ask staff to work an extra hour or get part time staff to extend their hours to cope with a 'blip' in demand. In the next section we'll look at the ability to respond to demand, but for now we'll focus on the ability to forecast what is needed and to plan work accordingly.

2.1 Responding to demand

Most organizations are driven by the demand for the goods or services they supply, whether they are in the public, private or voluntary sector. Sometimes this demand is relatively even throughout the year, but may be growing or declining over time. This is what is called the trend. Sometimes demand may fluctuate, with peaks and troughs at specific times. These are called seasonal variations. Others may suffer from unanticipated fluctuations due to events that could not be predicted (or, at least, not predicted when they would occur). For example:

- A hospital may have a constant demand for eye operations but with an upward trend as people live longer and suffer from age-related eye problems. It can also expect that demand for beds will be higher in winter (seasonal variation), as people suffer more from illnesses (especially older people) and injuries (more car crashes in dark, wet weather). It may also find itself inundated with patients due to a particularly virulent strain of 'flu – it can plan for such a sudden increase but doesn't know when or if it will occur.
- An insurance broker may have regular renewals of policies and new customers taking out policies at a fairly even rate, but with a slight downward trend in demand as more and more people buy over the Internet, but it always gets a surge in mid-summer and mid-winter when people change their cars with the change in licence plate numbers, causing them to have to change their insurance. The collapse of an online insurance company may suddenly create a surge of new business.

Activity 1

Think about your organization; what longer term trends can you see in what is supplied, both the volumes and the mix of different products or services?

_____

_____

Are there any seasonal variations in demand or supply? What causes these?

_____

_____

What could cause a sudden surge (or drop) in demand or the need to supply products or services?

_____

_____

2.2 Setting objectives

Most organizations make some effort to forecast what level of products or services they need to produce, and the mix of different types of product or service. They will often do this for at least the year ahead, often for two, three or more years, in outline. They will then plan in more detail for the four quarters of the current year, and the months of the current quarter and sometimes the weeks of the current month. This way they always have plans in increasing levels of detail for the current month and for the next four quarters.

These plans will usually translate into objectives for your team. These may be expressed in different ways depending on what you do. In manufacturing, they are most likely to be volumes of production, reject levels and the like. In services they may be customers served, sales made or processes completed.

If you have agreed your objectives and they are set out as SMART objectives, then you will know what you are expected to do. SMART objectives are Specific, so you know what is expected of you. They are Measurable, so you can judge how well you are meeting them. They are Achievable, so you believe that you are capable of meeting them (or you should not have agreed them). They are Relevant, which means that you can use them as the basis for planning what you are going to do, and they are Time bound, so that you have a clear time period within which to achieve them.

Your task is to convert these objectives into work plans and targets for your team.

3 What are you capable of doing?

The ability of your team to respond to variations in demand reflects various factors, mainly to do with the kind of resources you use, how people in your team are employed and their skills.

3.1 The resources you use

An oil refinery can only do one thing, refine oil, and operates on a *continuous production* basis. Some manufacturing and service organizations have a bit more flexibility but still operate 24 hours a day, most days of the week and most weeks of the year. They may be able to change what they produce but it takes time, because their *mass production* system is based on producing standard products although, in recent years, mass production has had to be come more able to produce greater variety, what has been described as *mass customization*.

Many more organizations operate on a *batch production* basis. This means that they produce varying quantities (batches) of different products or services. Others operate on a *project* or *commissioned production* basis, where each product or service is a one-off event, although they may be based on standard elements or components that are assembled together according to the work that needs to be done.

These differences in how organization operate will often reflect how easily they can expand or contract their production or supply of services, what economists call the elasticity of supply. Organizations which are capital-intensive (have large scale equipment, buildings and facilities) tend to have less flexibility (are less elastic in supply). They can't expand easily because they need to work near to full capacity to be economic, and can't add new capital easily.

Organizations which are labour-intensive (rely mainly on people) can more easily recruit to expand supply (are more supply elastic). However, this assumes that people are readily available, and have the skills needed. Some skills are in short supply, making it hard for organizations relying on them to increase output. Generally, the less you need specialist skills, the easier it is to find people to perform tasks.

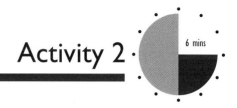

Activity 2

Think about your organization; how easily can it expand its production of products or services?

_____

_____

How capital or labour intensive is it? (There is no benchmark to use, but think of an oil refinery as the most capital intensive, and an agricultural labour contractor supplying fruit pickers as the most labour intensive.)

_____

_____

How dependent is you organization on specialist skills to supply products or services? Are they readily available or hard to find?

_____

_____

3.2 How people are employed

People can be working in an enormous variety of ways, but the main differences are between:

- Full-time, fractional, part-time and job-share
- Permanent, temporary or fixed term contract
- Fixed or flexible hours
- Shift or daytime only

Full-time, fractional, part-time and job-share employees

Over recent years, part-time workers have had their rights extended to the same basic conditions of employment as full-time workers, and many organizations benefit from being able to employ people to fit into variations in demand or cover for absent employees. Jobshare means that (usually) two employees fill one job role. Fractional posts are more substantial part-timers, usually working at least half the time of full time employees. Fractional, jobshare and part-time working has been more commonly taken up by women to enable them to combine work with childcare responsibilities, and this is one reason that rights have been extended, to prevent sex discrimination in employment.

The ability to employ people on a fractional or part-time basis means that you can expand or contract the level of activity in smaller steps, especially in labour-intensive operations. This makes it easier to respond to small changes in demand, but it can also lead to people being treated as second-class employees. You should always treat people who work less than the hours of full time workers as equal members of the work team in determining how work is planned and allocated.

Permanent, temporary or fixed term contract employees

Part time employees often get confused with temporary employees; they are not the same. Temporary employees, or people who are employed on fixed term contracts, are useful in covering for absent team members and coping with short term variations in demand. Some 'temps' are employed by agencies, others are directly employed. They are often treated as second class employees, not properly inducted and used poorly, yet they are often critical in enabling organizations to cope. In planning and allocating work to temporary or fixed term contract employees, take the time to find out what they are capable of and use them as effectively and efficiently as possible, to make it worthwhile employing them.

Fixed or flexible hours employees

Flexible working, or flexitime, has become increasingly common, as employers recognize the benefits of enabling people to work the hours that suit them. This can even out traffic congestion and reduce commuting stress. It can also help to extend the hours of operation by allowing people to come in earlier or stay later as it suits them. Fixed hours are really only needed if the whole team must work co-operatively or there is a need for full staffing during regular working hours. What flexible working can do is to make planning and allocating work a bit more problematic. However, by having clear guidelines on how the flexitime works and the importance of hitting work targets, you will get the benefits of more motivated team members without any significant disadvantages.

Shift or daytime only employees

There was a time when only factories and few other occupations worked shifts. Now, with a 24/7 culture and the growth of call centres, more and more people are working shifts. The original reason for shift working, and the reason it is still used in many capital-intensive industries, is to maximize the use of expensive capital. The reason why it is increasingly used now, however, is to ensure that an organization can supply goods or services at times that customers want them. Shift systems vary from continuous three shift operations, to organizations running short, early evening, (or 'twilight') shifts to operate an extended day.

Shift working can bring problems, with team members on different shifts not meeting and productivity varying on different shifts or after changes in shift patterns. Generally, people cannot work as well if their sleep patterns are disturbed. People working constant night shifts suffer because the natural circadian rhythms are based on sleeping at night, and have difficulty adjusting to different patterns of work and sleep.

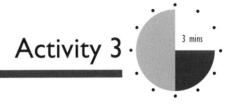

Activity 3

Which of these different employment patterns does your organization use? How do they affect the way that you plan and allocate work?

_____

_____

_____

_____

3.3 The skills people have

The resources you use and the way that people are employed are significant in determining how well your team can meet your work objectives. However, the third aspect is probably the most important of all, the skills that your team has.

Skills cover all aspects of team members' ability to perform, including their knowledge and their competence or ability to perform in their role, will reflect:

- their education and training
- their experience
- their attitudes and motivation
- their responsibility and control of their work.

Much of this workbook is concerned with these last two elements, because the most able employees can perform badly if they have a poor attitude to work, lack motivation, and feel undervalued and rigidly controlled in what they do. Conversely, someone with only adequate skills can improve in leaps and bounds if they are enthusiastic, properly motivated, given responsibility and control over their work. Ideally, you need to combine high skill levels with a work environment that brings the best out of people. The workbooks *Motivating to Perform in the Workplace* and *Developing Yourself and Others* focus on these aspects of your role.

4 Allocating work to people

In determining what each person should be doing you need to go through a five stage process:

1   Break down the team's or department's work objectives into specific targets, tasks or activities.

2   Rank these tasks in terms of priority, based on their *precedence*, *urgency* and *importance*. Precedence is the extent to which some tasks depend on the completion of others. A task that has to be completed before something else is done has precedence. Urgency is how soon the tasks need to be completed; importance is how significant the tasks are for achievement of overall goals.

3   Analyse the skills needed for completion of each task, bearing in mind that someone's skills reflect their education and training, experience, attitude, motivation, the ability to accept responsibility and take control.

4   List the skills of the team members, using these same dimensions. You should take account not just of someone's current skills level, but their development needs. Some tasks may serve to provide the experience that someone needs to develop their skill level, or allow someone to take on responsibility or help improve their motivation. Some tasks may also allow those with high skill levels to coach or mentor others to help bring them up to their standard.

5   Match people to the tasks.

A useful tool for doing this is a skills matrix. This is simple chart listing the main tasks in columns, with the specific skills requirements for each in sub-columns. Team members are listed down the side, in rows. For example:

Tasks / Skills / Teams members	Resolve customer service problems		
	Detailed knowledge of all products	Questioning and listening skills	Problem solving skills
A. Name			
B. Name			
C. Name			

It's possible to identify different stages of skills development:

- Not yet skilled
- Learning
- Skilled
- Coach

A coach is able to develop others, and pass on his or her high skill levels. A skills matrix like this makes it clear who is capable of dealing with any task.

Activity 4

Do you use a skills matrix, or anything like it? You may have one 'in your head', but it is better to use a formal matrix because that way you can discuss someone's current level of skills and their development plans.

_____

_____

_____

_____

4.1 Managing the gaps

In an ideal world there is a perfect match between the tasks and the people available to do them. Unfortunately, we don't live in an ideal world, which is why you often finish up with gaps between the tasks and the people. Gaps can mean that you have tasks without the right people, or people able to do more complex tasks than are needed. In the short term, the lack of appropriately skilled people is the hardest to solve.

Activity 5

What can you do if you have tasks and nobody able to perform them?

_____

_____

_____

_____

If the shortfall is due to inadequate levels of staff, then you are faced with having to recruit new people, either permanent or temporary, or sub-contract the work. If it is due to a skill shortage – you have the people but not the right skill mix – recruitment of new employees is not appropriate. Instead you will need to develop existing people. This is often the lowest cost solution to a skill gap, but too many organizations prefer to recruit new employees. On average it costs about one quarter of the first year's salary to recruit someone, and you can get a lot of training for that money. Added to which, training improves motivation and reduces labour staff turnover.

In the long term, under-using skilled people is the bigger problem. It is inefficient, as the organization is paying for skill it's not using. It is also likely to encourage people to lead, as they feel undervalued and under-stretched.

4.2 Planning your longer term labour needs

One of the tasks that first line managers are likely to be involved in is helping line managers to plan longer term labour needs. This is similar to the work allocation task, but on a longer time scale and in broader terms. It means looking at:

■ Forecasts of future work levels (outputs of products and services).
■ Forecasts of future labour productivity (how much each person can produce, on average). This will often have to take into account any planned investment in equipment, systems and training.
■ Forecasts of employee turnover (how many people you expect to leave, be promoted or retire).

You can do two simple sums based on this information:

1. $\dfrac{\text{Future work levels}}{\text{Future labour productivity}} = \text{Number of employees needed}$

Divide how much you will be expected to produce or do, per day/week/ month by the amount people can, on average, be expected to produce or do, per day/week/month. This tells you how many people you will need.

2. *Number of employees needed – (Current labour force – Forecast number leaving)*

Work out how many of the current labour force you will have in the period being discussed (which is the sum in brackets) and take this figure away from the forecast number you will need. The figure you have left is the number of people you will need to recruit or train up from elsewhere during this period to meet demand.

Activity 6

3 mins

In two years' time an organization expects to be processing 7,500 customer orders per week. It expects customer service people to be able to process 300 orders per week, a 25% increase on current levels. It currently employs 32 people, but three will retire in the next two years, and it usually loses at least three people a year to other jobs. How many people will it need to recruit or train up in the next two years?

_____

_____

_____

_____

The answer to this activity appears on page 106.

Of course, this is not always as easy as this makes it look. However, if you understand the basic principles you can work with managers on calculating the likely recruitment needs. One thing to note, however, is that you could finish up with a negative figure. If the *Number of employees needed* is less than the number you are likely to have *(Current labour force – Forecast number leaving)* this is the number that will have to be made redundant.

5 Controlling people

Can people be controlled?

Experience tells us that, in normal working life, managers cannot – and, if they are sensible, don't even attempt to – control every action of the people they manage.

Getting team members to meet objectives and to follow standards is not so much a matter of control as of **motivation.**

Activity 7

3 mins

In your own words, describe what you understand by 'motivation'.

_____

_____

_____

_____

_____

_____

Motivation is about getting people to **want** to do things, rather than trying to **make** them do things.

One of the best ways to motivate people to work well is to allow them to have responsibility and control over their **own** work. Imposing stringent controls usually has the effect of making others less well motivated.

So you could define the task of a team leader as finding the right compromise between the two extremes of attempting to keep every activity under strict personal supervision, and allowing team members to do as they please.

You want to monitor events and activities, because you may need to take action when things start going wrong. Yet if the team feel that they can't do anything without checking with you first, they may feel undervalued and demoralized.

The trick is to build up **mutual trust and understanding**, and to help create an atmosphere in which everyone wants to make a positive contribution.

5.1 Creating the right atmosphere

If you've been lucky enough to have had the experience of being in a group where there is a pleasant, friendly and open climate or atmosphere, you will know how effective such a group can be. It's often because:

- members support each other and stand up for each other;
- there is real communication;
- people seem to care about the standards of the group;
- everyone's views are listened to, and everyone's efforts are appreciated.

Perhaps you agree that this is the kind of atmosphere every workteam should aim for.

It can't be done overnight, and takes a lot of effort. But it's well worthwhile working at it.

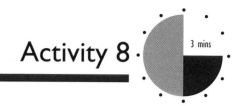

Activity 8 · 3 mins

What can a first line manager do to help develop this kind of positive atmosphere?

Choose the preferable option from each pair listed below.

a Tell the team not only what they need to know to do the job, but the background to the work – why it's needed, who the customers are, what will be the effects of getting it wrong, and so on. ☐ OR b Use the 'need to know' principle. Tell the team enough to do the job to the required standard and no more, on the basis that anything else is none of their concern. ☐

c Discourage discussion, unless it's relevant to the job in hand. ☐ OR d Encourage discussion about any aspect of the work, the organization and the team. ☐

e Give responsibility to all team members, as far as you think they are able to handle it. ☐ OR f Retain as much of the responsibility for yourself as you can. ☐

g Show the standards of work you expect and stamp hard on any failures. ☐ OR h Give recognition and praise freely and generously. Show that you appreciate the work they do. ☐

l Don't get involved in the lives and interests of the team; who are you to interfere? ☐ OR j Make it your job to get to know every individual and to find out what makes him or her 'tick' – without intruding into private matters. ☐

You would have done well to choose responses a, d, e, h and j. If you read these paragraphs again, you may agree that they represent what might be called the 'open and trusting' approach.

However, you may not totally agree with this approach. You might point out that some groups work well together with a leader who is dour and unbending, who achieves results by setting high standards for himself or herself and expecting others to do the same. We all have our own style. There is no such thing as a fixed set of rules for motivating people.

5.2 Job enrichment

These days, organizations are tending to move away from the tradition of breaking jobs down into simple and (often) menial tasks. There is a growing acceptance of the fact that most people:

- will take a much more positive attitude to work if they're given the opportunity to use their skills and talents to the full;
- are quite capable of handling responsibility;
- are much more productive when they enjoy what they're doing.

Activity 9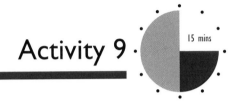

Here are some ideas for enriching jobs. Read it through and for each point, say what you might do to apply the concept to your own team and work situation:

- Let individual team members see a whole job through from start to finish, rather than breaking the job down into small tasks.

_____

_____

_____

_____

- Increase the level of responsibility for the job wherever and whenever possible.

_____

_____

_____

_____

- Reduce the level of supervision, giving team members greater control over the way they approach a job, the equipment they need and so on.

_____

_____

_____

_____

■ Increase the range of tasks which you delegate.

_____

_____

_____

_____

■ Give individuals every opportunity to become expert in some specific task or sphere of activity.

_____

_____

_____

_____

■ Seek to widen the scope of jobs for which you and your team are responsible.

_____

_____

_____

_____

■ Make sure that jobs are meaningful and that team members can see their relevance.

_____

_____

_____

_____

There are many possible answers to these questions, and yours will apply only to your own circumstances. For example, you might have written, in response to 'Increase the level of responsibility for the job wherever and whenever possible':

■ 'Hazel could take responsibility for checking that new jobs are allocated a number, and are entered on the tracking software.'
Or, in your response to 'Seek to widen the scope of jobs for which you and your team are responsible':

■ 'I don't see why we could not give candidates a preliminary interview, to save the time of senior staff, and weed out the really unsuitable ones.'

5.3 Training and development

A workteam is a wonderful animal. Unlike most equipment, it can be trained and developed to adapt to changing demands and new situations.

You are probably carrying out training all the time. Each time you explain a new process or answer a query, you are adding to the workteam's knowledge. As tasks are performed, team members gradually become more proficient.

Perhaps you have more formal responsibilities for training as well. Whether you run formal training courses yourself, or leave it to a specialist, you play a large part in **recognizing training needs**, and **selecting people for particular training.**

Activity 10 · 3 mins

Introducing a new piece of equipment is one situation that would suggest a need for training. Try to think of **two** others.

_____

_____

_____

_____

Some examples are as follows:

- an increase in accident rate
- materials being wasted   } Specific performance problems.
- low output
- poor quality

- introducing a new method
- introducing new equipment   } Changes in work patterns.
- starting a new kind of task

- wanting to give an individual
  the chance to develop
- needing to fill a skills gap
- planning to expand the team's
  activities.

  $\Big\}$ Broadening skills.

Training can provide new opportunities for individuals, for the team and for the team leader.

To summarize this section, four points can be made.

- Controlling work effectively is not only a matter of organizing and employing specific techniques – it is also about getting the team to **want** to achieve objectives and to measure up to high standards.
- The better the atmosphere, and the greater the understanding between team members, the more likely it is that work will be successful and under control.
- Job enrichment is one, very significant, approach to motivation and increased productivity.
- Training can give the workteam the chance to develop and broaden its skill base.

The key to controlling work is in managing and motivating the people.

Self-assessment 1 ·

15 mins

1 Changes in the level of demand or output of products or services over time are caused by upward or downward _____, _____ variations and _____ variations.

2 In determining what your team is capable of doing, in term of workload, you need to take account of _____, the way that _____ _____ and their _____.

3 The five stages in allocating work to people are:

1. _____

2. _____

3. _____

4. _____

5. _____

4 The number of employees needed in future can be calculated by the formula:

   _____

5 The number of people you will need to recruit or make redundant at a future point in time can be calculated by the formula:

   _____ − (_____ − _____)

6 How could you recognize what kind of atmosphere – the general feeling or mood – existed in a workplace?

7 Fill in the blanks in the following statements with suitable words chosen from the list underneath.

   ■ Controlling work effectively is not only a matter of _____ and employing specific _____ – it is also about getting the team to _____ to achieve objectives and to _____ up to high standards.

   ■ The better the _____, and the greater the _____ between team members, the more likely it is that work will be successful and under _____.

   ■ Job _____ is one, very significant, approach to _____ and increased _____.

   ■ _____ can give the workteam the chance to _____ and broaden its _____ base.

   ■ The key to controlling work is in managing and _____ the people.

ATMOSPHERE	CONTROL	DEVELOP
ENRICHMENT	MEASURE	MOTIVATING
MOTIVATION	ORGANIZING	PRODUCTIVITY
SKILL	TECHNIQUES	TRAINING
UNDERSTANDING	WANT	

Answers to these questions can be found on page 103.

6 Summary

- Most organizations have changes or fluctuations in demand or work output. These are:

    - Upward or downward trends
    - Seasonal variations
    - Unanticipated variations

- Organizations make some effort to forecast what level and mix of products or services they need to produce for at least the year ahead, and in more detail for the four quarters of the current year, and the months of the current quarter. These plans will usually translate into objectives for your team.

- The ability of your team to respond to variations in demand reflects the kind of resources you use, how people in your team are employed and their skills.

- In determining what each person should be doing you need to go through a five stage process:

    1. Break down the objectives into specific targets, tasks or activities.
    2. Rank these tasks in terms of priority.
    3. Analyse the skills needed for each task.
    4. List the skills of the team members.
    5. Match people to the tasks.

- You can help to plan longer term labour needs by looking at:

    - Forecasts of future work levels
    - Forecasts of future labour productivity
    - Forecasts of employees

- You can control how well people complete tasks by motivating them through:

    - Creating the right atmosphere
    - Enriching jobs
    - Training and development

Session B
Delegation – a vital skill

1 Introduction

Effective delegation enables you to get work done through other people and is central to effective management.

In recent years we have seen changes in the way work is organized. Organizations and workteams have become 'lean', but a lean workteam is no use unless it is flexible and able to respond quickly to new circumstances. So it is athletic workteams we need, not skeletons! Being flexible means being capable of being deployed where you are most needed. Delegating to your team means that you build up a pool of experience and skill which you can use in a flexible way. It also enables you to cope with pressure at work, when your organization asks you to achieve more in your work.

In this session we'll look at what is involved in delegating, and we will demonstrate that its practice is a skill, and as such can be both learned and improved.

Poorly managed delegation can lead people to think that delegation means someone is 'passing the buck', or just getting someone else to do their work for them. We'll see why effective delegation could not be further from this dismissive description. We'll show how it is an important technique to use for managing your team successfully.

2 What does delegation mean?

Giving a definition of delegation may seem a bit like trying to define 'electricity'. Although it is fairly easy to see what it can do for you, it is difficult to describe what it is in words. Still, we need to start this session by knowing and agreeing what we are talking about. So what does delegation mean to you?

Activity 11

Spend a little time thinking about delegation, perhaps your experience of delegation or delegation that you have observed at work. Then write down in a few lines what you think it means.

_____

_____

_____

We have already said that some people regard delegation as passing the buck, but let's hope you have found a more positive description.

I would define delegation in the following way.

■ Delegation means giving someone else the responsibility and authority to act on your behalf.

You may have used different words in your description and still be correct. The important words are **responsibility** and **authority** and we will come back to these later.

So, if you delegate, you ask somebody else to **do** something or to make something happen, much as you normally do in your job.

You will know from your own experience that to make something happen at work you need resources of some kind. If you delegate a certain responsibility, then the member of your team who takes on that responsibility will need resources too, and you will have to think through how they are to be allocated.

Activity 12

5 mins

What are the resources which a manager has to allocate? List at least three in the space below.

_____

_____

_____

Which of these do you think is the most important?

_____

I hope we can agree that the resources which managers can allocate include equipment and materials, finance, information, time and people.

In most situations, people are the most important resource. People bring their skills and expertise to act on other resources in order to achieve results. Without their co-operation nothing will happen.

So delegation means negotiating agreement with other people in order to:

- give them **responsibility** to act on your behalf;
- give them the **authority** needed to get the job done;
- allocate **resources** to them – including other people – that are needed to get the job done.

3 Why is it important to delegate?

As a first line manager your organization has given you the authority to use resources to achieve results. For example, you use information from team members and from senior managers to make decisions and take action. You can share some of this authority with team members so they too can achieve results.

Delegating responsibility to team members can be one of the most helpful things you can do for them.

Effective delegation benefits team members in the following ways.

- Delegation helps people to develop new skills and competence and so demonstrate their ability.
- It helps people become more involved and trusted at work and to feel that they are valued members of the team.
- It gives people a wider and more varied experience at work than they might otherwise get.
- It enables people to find out more about what is going on.
- It helps staff to feel empowered and increases their commitment.

> 'True delegation, effective delegation, is delegation with trust and with only the necessary minimum of controls.'
>
> Charles Handy
> *Understanding Organizations* (1999, p. 284).

Successful delegation helps to **develop** team members who are competent, involved, committed and well-informed. Such team members are likely to perform highly – a real asset to any organization.

By using delegation to help their team members, managers are also helping themselves – for you'll probably agree it is easier to work with a well-motivated competent team, than with a group of people who are reluctant to do the work and are not interested in what they are doing.

But delegation is also an important management technique for at least four other reasons. It helps managers to:

- make better decisions;
- make the most of their own limited time;
- keep control of a large team;
- improve the team's overall performance.

Let's look at these in turn.

3.1 Making better decisions

As a team leader your role is to manage your team and the work it does. To do so effectively you need to make good decisions about all aspects of the work of the team.

Activity 13

3 mins

What do you think is needed if good decisions are to be made?

_____

_____

You may have mentioned the importance of reliable, up-to-date and complete information. I would argue that you need to have access to quality information in order to make a good decision.

As a team leader you are at the centre of a network of communications with information flowing from you and to you in all directions (see diagram). Your management perspective gives you an overview of what is going on – something which possibly none of your workteam quite shares. The better the flow of information, the better you can plan, organize and control the work for which you are responsible.

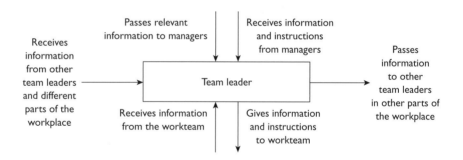

'All decisions should be made as low as possible in the organization. The Charge of the Light Brigade was ordered by an officer who wasn't there looking at the territory.'

Robert Townsend, author of _Up the Organization._

But even in the best-run teams there are bound to be gaps in the team leader's store of information. In fact, the more teams are encouraged to take responsibility for their own work, to develop their own skills and to take a real interest in all aspects of the job, the greater becomes the detailed information and knowledge available within the team and the smaller the proportion of it that the team leader will know. It is simply a fact of life that the team leader is not going to know everything. Part of the reason for this is that detailed knowledge comes with actually doing the job and that is not what team leaders are usually paid for. Their job is to get the job done through other people.

Delegation is a way of tapping into the detailed knowledge and information within your team and bringing these to bear upon specific tasks or projects. By encouraging your team to contribute the detailed information you may well lack, you will have more confidence that your management decisions are sound. Greater participation by staff can be a real source of solid support on a day-to-day basis.

3.2 Effective use of limited time

Most managers have more work to do than they have time for, and very often feel that some of their work never gets done or doesn't get the attention it deserves. Delegation allows managers to balance their workload.

■ Managers can delegate the low to medium priority jobs to others and, by doing so, make sure that the jobs get done properly.
■ With the time saved by giving some of their work to others, they will have more time to work on the high priority jobs and the work which only they can do.

Although the process of delegation takes time, bear in mind that it is time spent **developing team members and giving them an opportunity to grow**. This is an important management responsibility. So delegation represents effective use of a manager's time.

3.3 Keeping control

'Span of control' is a term used to describe the number of members in a workteam for which a particular manager is responsible. That is, it states the number of people under their control.

We'll look at what this means in practice.

Activity 14

Alex works for a large insurance company and is responsible for a sales team of forty. Recently the company brought in a new bonus scheme linked to the amount of new work each salesperson obtained. This resulted in the sales team increasing their individual business by an average of 25%. As a consequence, Alex's own workload increased considerably and the office work has begun to get into a bit of a mess.

Alex was called into the sales manager's office and asked to explain why things had got out of control lately. The manager suggested that Alex needed to take a course in office management so as to be better able to cope with the work. Alex's response to this was to say that what was needed was not more training but fewer people to supervise.

Which of these two suggestions do you think is more likely to solve Alex's problem?

_____

_____

I expect you agree that Alex's problem is not likely to be a lack of training, but too large a span of control. It is always going to be difficult to control a team of forty without having assistance.

There is no definite 'best' number of people that a first line manager can control, but some management experts have suggested that it can be as high as twelve, provided these people do not themselves supervise others. Much depends on the circumstances, such as the nature of the job, the time available for direct supervision, the character of the workteam and the amount of training received.

What is clear is that the greater the number of people in a workteam, the more difficult it is for their manager to keep control.

Delegation is a major way of coping with a large a span of control, and it is the reason why organizations use 'family-tree'-type structures, that look like this.

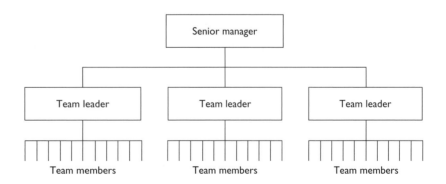

The workforce is divided into teams, usually with a team leader or first line manager responsible for a relatively small number of people.

Delegating work is one important way to help you keep effective control of a large group of people. By using delegation, you can give each member of your workteam responsibility for making sure their own part of the group's work fits into place. This encourages greater commitment and participation, essential elements of successful teamwork.

In this way a workteam is rather like an orchestra – each section, such as the strings, percussion, and so on, is responsible for its own part of the musical score – with you playing the role of conductor and being responsible for bringing all the parts together for a perfect performance.

3.4 Improving the team's performance

'Management, above everything else, is about people. It is about the accomplishment of ends and aims by the efforts of groups of people working together.'

Sir John Harvey-Jones.

To improve the way your team works you need to bring together the individual contributions of the people in your workteam so that they form a united group, working towards the same ends. This involves:

- getting to know each team member – their strengths and weaknesses, their personal aims and ambitions, what aspects of their work they enjoy and dislike and so on;
- making sure the goals and objectives of the team are understood and shared by everyone;
- planning to make the best use of each team member so that everyone is fully committed to the team effort.

Activity 15 · 5 mins

How do you think delegating work can actually improve team performance?

_____

_____

_____

_____

Delegation gives you the opportunity to make the most of the individuals in your team and to show that you value them and their work. You can improve the team's performance by delegating in two different ways.

EXTENSION 1
As a team leader you need to motivate your team members. To find out more about motivation, see Extension 1 on page 101.

■ You can **build on the strengths of each team member**. If one person is better at a certain type of work than others, it makes sense to use that strength by delegating that particular job to him or her. In this way you improve the team's commitment.

■ On the other hand you may plan to use delegation to **develop the skills of an individual team member**. Here you are demonstrating confidence that the individual has the potential to develop new skills, thus increasing their opportunities to participate, and you are working to improve the pool of skills in the team.

Activity 16 · 10 mins

Think about what you have learned about the importance of delegating, and give at least one reason why delegating is important to the following people.

■ Team leaders.

_____

_____

■ Team members.

_____

_____

■ Organizations.

_____

_____

With effective delegation, everybody wins.

Delegation enables team leaders to:

■ develop a committed and motivated team;
■ develop the skills of individuals;
■ draw on the expertise of their team members;
■ make better decisions;
■ make effective use of their own time;
■ co-ordinate and control a team;
■ improve the performance of the team.

Effective delegation can help individual team members to:

- increase their skills and expertise;
- get a variety of experience, increasing their opportunities to participate;
- feel that they are trusted and valued members of the team, which encourages greater commitment;
- increase their knowledge about the organization and the work of the team as a whole.

Delegation can promote a competent, committed, enthusiastic and well-informed workforce, and this is obviously important to any organization. But delegation is also important to organizations because it increases the flow of information at all levels, and effective communications throughout an organization are essential for good decision making.

4 Objections to delegating

We have seen some of the main reasons why delegation is an important technique, bringing benefits to team members, team leaders and the organization as a whole.

But some team leaders seem to be rather reluctant to pass on work to members of their workteam.

Activity 17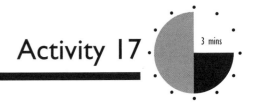

Jot down one or two reasons for reluctance to delegate work.

_____

_____

_____

_____

You could have thought of a number of possibilities. The first ones that strike me are the following.

■ People may think that it's quicker to do the job themselves, or find that they are not satisfied with the quality of job that one of their workteam would do, and so prefer to do the job themselves.

■ As we have already mentioned, delegation demands that you make resources available, and in an attempt to protect their position of authority, some people like to keep resources – especially information – to themselves.

■ People may feel that asking somebody else to do something implies that they are not able to do it themselves and are not really up to the job.

■ They may not trust the workteam and may feel that delegation of work means it is going outside their control.

Although we may recognize these concerns, we will see in this workbook that they do not represent sound reasons for reluctance to delegate. They suggest, instead, a misunderstanding about what delegation actually involves. We'll look at this in some detail, but first let's return to the ideas of authority and responsibility that are at the core of delegating.

5 Authority and responsibility

We have already suggested that delegation happens when, as a team leader, you negotiate with a member of your workteam to give them the authority to do something on your behalf. At the same time, you have made them **responsible** for doing the job.

However, this doesn't mean that you can pass responsibility to them for seeing that the job gets done properly, and on time.

If you give a team member the **authority** to do something, you may be losing some authority, since you no longer make the decisions – they are made by the team member instead. But when you give authority to the team member, you do not lose any **responsibility** – if anything you increase it. Although the team member is responsible for doing the job, you are responsible both for getting it done and for trusting the team member to do it. So delegation means you **lose** some authority, but both you and the team member **gain** responsibility.

In the end the **overall responsibility** is yours – after all, that's what managers and team leaders are paid for. Otherwise you have given up your job altogether, rather than just delegating a part of it.

5.1 Responsibility and accountability

Who are you
accountable to in
your organization?
And who is
accountable to you?

These terms are often used interchangeably, but in fact they mean different things. It helps to think of them as 'responsibility for' and 'accountability to' in order to perceive the distinction. As we've seen, there are things about your job that you are always responsible for, including the outcome of the delegated tasks. However, your job in the organization's hierarchy inevitably means that you are **accountable to** or **answerable to** someone else higher up the line of authority. This is why you can never relinquish ultimate responsibility, because it is you who will have to answer for the consequences of any actions that you take.

> Peter was managing a large publishing project for a client. The workload turned out to be much heavier than he had anticipated, and in order to meet the deadline, he sub-contracted part of the work to another freelance colleague, Gerry. Despite Peter's careful instructions, Gerry made what Peter described as 'a complete pig's ear' of the job. 'It just wasn't possible to send the work back to the client,' he said to a friend. 'They would have just flung it back in my face. And you can't say, "Well, it's not my fault, someone else made a mess of it." It was up to me to make sure it was sent off to the client in an acceptable state. So I worked day and night for several days to make sure it was. It was me who would have to explain to the client why the work was in a mess, not Gerry, because I was ultimately responsible for the job, not him.'

5.2 Authority and power

Authority also gives power. Your authority as a manager gives you power to influence other people. One definition of power is 'the means of influencing the thoughts and actions of others.' The higher up the organization people are, the more power and influence they have. This is **position power**, and we'll look at it briefly here. Your job as a manager gives you position power.

There are different degrees of position power, depending on how high up you are in the organization. The managing director will have a great deal more position power than a first line manager. He or she will be able to influence many more people's thoughts and actions and to a much greater extent.

There are various strategies you can employ as a supervisor to influence your staff. Some will be particularly effective when your position power is high. Others will depend more on using **personal power**. These strategies include:

- **assertiveness** – used most frequently when position power is high but success will be difficult to achieve;
- **friendliness** – often used when both position power and expectations of success are low;
- **reason** – used frequently when position power and expectations of success are high;
- **referral** to a higher authority;
- **sanctions** or **disciplinary action**.

You'll often use more than one strategy, but you should aim to avoid using the last two unless absolutely necessary.

> Deena had been recently promoted to a managerial position. At first she felt uncomfortable in the role because she was no longer at the same level as her colleagues, with whom she'd been very friendly, and she felt they no longer regarded her in the same way as before. She tried adopting the strategy of asking them to do things in a friendly way. Although this worked part of the time, if it was a case of asking someone to do an unpopular task, it was more difficult to get anyone to agree. They'd make a joke of it and make excuses as to why they couldn't do it, and she spent a lot of time trying to persuade people to no avail. Eventually Deena went on an assertiveness training course, and now has a much better idea of how to use her personal power in an assertive way to get things done.

Activity 18

15 mins

Jot down what you see as the difference in the responsibility for a job between a team leader and a member of their workteam to whom they have delegated it.

_____

_____

_____

Richard E. Krafve, President of Raytheon Corporation put the issue of authority and responsibility succinctly.

'You can delegate authority, but you can never delegate responsibility by delegating a task to someone else.'

I hope you agree that the difference is that the workteam member has the responsibility for doing the job, but that the team leader is responsible for seeing that it gets done, properly and on time.

In other words, as a team leader, you must stay in overall **control** of the work.

One reason people are often reluctant to delegate is the fear of losing power. If I have the power to make something happen and I give it to you I may be fearful of losing that power, yet still having responsibility for the decisions you make in my name. You gain power and I lose it, without any balancing gain, as I am still accountable to those who gave me the power. This idea of power is very short-sighted. It is based on the idea of power from a battery, a generator or an engine. By linking a light bulb to a battery, a winch to a generator or fitting an engine in a vehicle, we use up the power they produce. There is no more power to share. This is called a zero-sum, because the power added to one application is matched by the power taken away. They cancel each other out, or add up to zero.

However, instead of thinking of mechanical or electrical power, think instead of kindness. If I am kind to you and that encourages you to be kind to others, I don't become less kind. I don't have a stock of kindness that reduces as I use it. In fact, by being kind to others I increase the stock of kindness in the world. Personal power is like this; the more we allow others to make decisions, the more power we create. This is called non-zero sum, because adding power doesn't take it away. You still possess the power you delegated, but so does the person you delegated it to.

You have also increased accountability, because the person with the delegated power becomes accountable to you for the way they use it, and you stay accountable for the power you still possess. Accountability is non-zero sum as well. The more power is delegated down, the more power there is, and the more accountability there is as well. If you delegate effectively, you will stay in overall control. Let's see what's involved in effective delegation.

6 The process of delegation

To delegate effectively you need to take time to prepare to delegate and then go on to carry out the delegation.

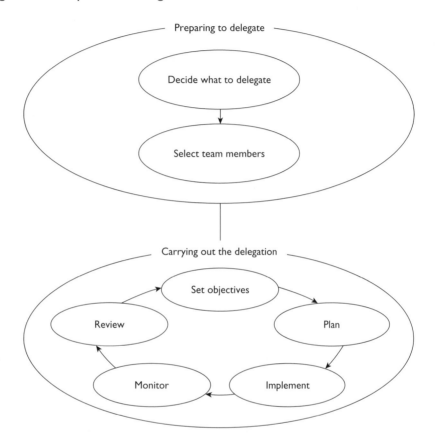

In **preparing to delegate** you look at the overall picture of your work, and the workload, competence and needs of team members. You will decide:

■ what tasks, activities and duties you can delegate;
■ to which of your team members you delegate these to.

We look at preparing to delegate in Session C.

To carry out the delegation you need to do the following.

■ **Set and agree the objectives**. In other words, what do you want the person to whom you are delegating to achieve?

■ **Plan** the delegation by:

  ■ allocating appropriate resources – in other words, what resources are needed to achieve the objectives, including support from you;

- deciding how to keep track of progress – for example, at what stages will the person taking on the task report to you;

- briefing the team member and agreeing the way forward, and agreeing milestones, in other words what will be achieved when.

■ **Let the team member implement** the delegated task – when the team member begins to do the work, you take a back seat while still providing support and controlling the work in the ways you have agreed.

■ **Monitor** the delegated task – both you and the person carrying out the delegation will need to keep an eye on progress, to ensure the task is going according to plan and going to meet the objectives, and then taking action, where appropriate to ensure the task stays on course.

■ **Review** the delegated task with the team member when it is completed by:

- evaluating what went well and what aspects could be improved next time;
- giving helpful feedback to the team member to improve future performance.

Notice that these stages – setting objectives, planning, implementing, monitoring and reviewing – tend to form a continuous cycle. This is because when you have completed the review stage you are then ready to set new or revised objectives. As a team leader you may be familiar with this cycle which is used for planning and controlling many work activities.

We will look in more detail at the stages of carrying out the delegation in Session D.

Activity 19

5 mins

You have looked briefly at what's involved in delegating effectively. Write a checklist of the things team leaders must do to meet their responsibilities when delegating tasks to their team. We have given the first one to start you off.

When delegating team leaders need to:

■ decide which of their tasks they can delegate;

_____

_____

_____

_____

_____

_____

Your checklist should show that team leaders need to prepare for delegating by deciding what to delegate and who to delegate to. They then need to set objectives and plan the delegation. They need to support the team member who is carrying out the delegated task and monitor the task in the ways that have been agreed. Finally, they need to review the delegation with the team member, providing appropriate feedback and considering how to make improvements next time. By using the process of delegation, team leaders meet their responsibilities for getting the job done properly.

7 Levels of control in delegation

In delegating effectively you will stay in overall control. However, as a manager you can choose an appropriate level of control to match:

- your preferred approach;
- the skills, experience and attitudes of your team members;
- the constraints of the job.

In general, the level of control managers use in delegation will relate to the extent to which they trust their team members to do a good job. You can see the relationship between trust and control in this graph.

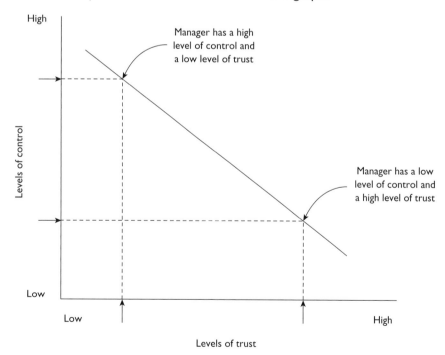

Managers who have a high degree of trust in team members are likely to feel they need to take little direct control of the work themselves.

For example, when a manager gives a team member a high level of responsibility for the delegated task, the team member is able to make his or her own decisions as to method, timing, resources and so on, although he or she will usually discuss these decisions with the manager, and the manager may offer guidance, advice and support.

Here is how one manager explains how she controls her team.

> 'I find the best way to keep things under control is to make sure my team know what we need to achieve and the importance of working to company regulations and procedures. I make sure they know they can come to me to discuss ideas and explore possibilities. Then I leave them to carry on with the job, only checking that it is going OK in an informal way.'

When managers have a low level of confidence or trust in team members they are likely to take a high level of direct control of the work, and limit the responsibility they give to each person. For example, they may tell the team member how to do the job, and ask for regular and routine progress reports at various stages.

Whatever level of control is used, it is important to bear in mind that, since nobody is perfect, some mistakes are bound to be made by your team. However, this should not stop you delegating to them.

Activity 20

How do you feel when someone shows that they trust you to do something on their behalf?

_____

_____

How do you feel when someone asks you to do something, but then doesn't let you get on with it, and clearly doesn't trust you to get it right?

_____

_____

I think most people feel committed to doing a good job when they are entrusted with it. They are likely to put in the effort required to get it right. But when they know they aren't expected to do a good job, most people would lack motivation, commitment and interest in the work.

Showing you trust your team is important if they are to give their best to a job. However, trust is a quality which grows and develops through experience and over time.

If you do not yet have confidence in team members' abilities, you can use careful delegation to **build trust**. Bear in mind that the process of delegation helps you to develop the skills of your team members.

Use high levels of control when you delegate tasks at first. By doing this, you can give appropriate advice and support whenever you feel the team member needs help. In this way you make it more likely that the team member will succeed. When the team member succeeds in carrying out tasks, you will have more confidence to gradually release direct control, giving that individual more responsibility to do a good job, and showing more trust in them.

Remember that you – as manager – retain overall responsibility for a job you have delegated. In the next two sessions we look at how to do this by going through the process of delegation.

8 How effective delegation will help you

We have seen that with delegation everybody wins, and we have looked at the stages involved in delegating effectively. Before we look at the particular advantages you are likely to gain from effective delegation, work through the next activity.

Activity 21

15 mins

Answer Yes or No to each of the following questions.

1   Do you spend time doing things which you think other people in your workteam could do for you?   **YES**   **NO**

2   Do you find that a number of tasks on your list of jobs cannot be placed under the headings of planning, organizing, motivating, developing or controlling, creating and communicating?   **YES**   **NO**

3   Do you work on jobs which you like to do, although others in your workteam could do them just as well, if not better?   **YES**   **NO**

4   Do you find yourself frequently interrupted by telephone calls which could just as easily be dealt with by someone else?   **YES**   **NO**

5   If you are temporarily away from your workteam, do they have to delay decisions until you come back?   **YES**   **NO**

6   Do you find that others seldom reach the high standards you set for them?   **YES**   **NO**

7   At the end of the day, do you have a number of unfinished tasks which you feel should have been done?   **YES**   **NO**

8   Is it difficult for you to find time to consult with your workteam regularly?   **YES**   **NO**

9   Do you keep information about work tasks to yourself on the grounds that, as supervisor, you ought to know things the rest of your team don't need to know?   **YES**   **NO**

10   Do you feel that in general you are overworked?   **YES**   **NO**

11   Do you have problems with access to the information or contacts you need to make decisions?   **YES**   **NO**

12   Are you slowed down by the lack of authority to make decisions?   **YES**   **NO**

The answers you have given to questions 1–10 should help you to make your own case for delegating effectively. They should show you what advantages you might gain from delegating to your workteam.

Think about the advantages which you most want to gain from delegating. You will need to identify these for your personal development plan.

If you answered 'Yes' to either question 11 or 12, you need to ask yourself 'Is it within my knowledge and authority to do this?' If your answer is 'No', then you may have a case for upward delegation. So far we have tended to look at delegation in terms of the tasks and responsibilities you delegate to your team. But when you think about your team, you should also include your own line manager. It may simply be more effective occasionally to pass a specific task upwards than to attempt to do it yourself or pass it downwards.

To gain advantages from delegation – whether down to your team or upwards to your line manager – you must become an effective delegator. We will look at the skills involved in delegating in the next sessions, and you will have an opportunity to practise using these skills in your workplace.

In this session we have looked at the meaning of delegation, and at the reasons why it is important to delegate to your team. We have introduced the process of effective delegation, which involves preparing for the delegation – deciding what and to whom to delegate and then carrying it out through the activities of setting objectives, planning, implementing, monitoring and reviewing. You have looked at your own situation, and at how delegating could benefit you. By now you should have an idea of the advantages you want to gain through effective delegation.

Self-assessment 2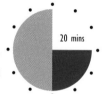

20 mins

For questions 1 to 6 complete the sentences with a suitable word or words.

1 Delegation means giving someone _____ and _____ to act on your behalf.

2 If a task is delegated to you, you also need _____ allocated to you in order to carry it out.

3 When you delegate a task, you have _____ _____ for seeing that a job is done properly and on time.

4   Successful delegation helps to develop team members who are _____,
    _____, _____ and _____.

5   Delegation enables team leaders to draw on the expertise of team members
    and so improve _____ _____.

6   Give two reasons why delegating represents an effective use of your time.

    _____

    _____

    _____

    _____

7   What does 'span of control' mean?

    _____

    _____

8   Complete the following diagram to show the process of delegation.

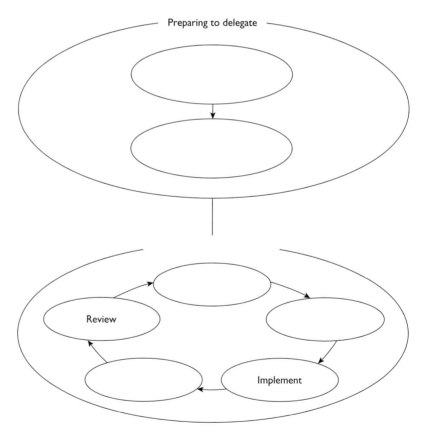

9 Complete the following sentence with the appropriate words.

The level of _____ you decide to take when you delegate is related to how much you _____ the person to do a good job.

10 How can you develop trust through delegating?

_____

_____

Answers to these questions can be found on page 104.

9 Summary

- Delegation means giving someone else the **responsibility** to act for you and the **authority** to do it.

- **Authority** confers **power**, which may in practice flow from the position (position power) or from the person who holds it (personal power).

- Delegation helps to make team members well-informed **participants**, who are competent, involved and **committed**.

- **Delegation** is an important management technique to use to:

  - make better decisions;
  - make effective use of time;
  - keep control of a large team;
  - improve the performance of the team.

- The ultimate responsibility for seeing that a job is done properly and on time is the team leader's.

- Managers are **responsible for** the tasks and the people over whom they have authority; they are **accountable to** the person in authority over them.

- To keep **control** of a delegated task you need to delegate effectively as follows.

  - **Prepare** for delegation by choosing an appropriate task and selecting an appropriate person.
  - **Carry out** the delegation by:
    setting clear objectives;
    planning;
    implementing;
    monitoring;
    reviewing.

- **Review the delegation**.

- The level of direct control you take in delegating is related to the amount of **trust** you have that the person who will carry out the delegated task will do a good job.

- You can develop trust in team members by going carefully through the process of delegation and helping the team member to be successful by using an appropriate level of **control**.

Session C
Preparing to delegate

█●█ 1 Introduction

In this session and in Session D we examine the process of effective delegation and ask you to apply the process in your work by delegating a suitable task to one of your team members. If you are not yet in a position to delegate, you will still find it useful to work through the sessions now, but plan to work through them again when you come to delegate tasks.

The skills of delegation include knowing what to delegate and to which member of your workteam.

In this session we will look in general terms at what parts of a team leader's job can be delegated; then you will look at your own work to select particular tasks that you can delegate and select a real task which you want to delegate.

Delegation can be a way of demonstrating that you recognize the skills of a particular team member, or the enthusiasm and commitment they possess. Depending on the type of task you delegate, it can also be part of a system of rewards, for example, if you delegate a desirable task rather than one that may be low priority or routine.

The success of delegation depends to a large extent on your choosing the most appropriate person to take on the job. To make this judgement you must get to know the strengths and weaknesses of team members. In the second half of this session you will choose an appropriate team member for the delegated task.

2 What should not be delegated?

There are clearly parts of any manager's job that cannot be delegated. It is important to identify these activities first and separate them from the others. You can then look at these other jobs and assess which are most suitable for delegating.

Work which is of a confidential nature should not be delegated. Similarly, team leaders cannot delegate tasks for which they do not have the authority in the first place. Nor can they delegate **all** their authority, or they will have passed over the job altogether.

Your company regulations and policies may specify jobs which only you can do, or there may be procedures which only you can undertake.

Activity 22

Think about your own particular job and write down **two** things which you cannot delegate, and why this is.

_____

_____

Your answers will depend on your own circumstances, but here are some examples of work activities that you would not delegate:

■ disciplinary action;
■ counselling staff;
■ reviewing the performance of team members;
■ your role in promoting health and safety at work;
■ planning and organizing the work activities of the whole team.

3 What should be delegated?

We'll now consider which tasks you ought to delegate to your workteam.

Activity 23

You are the office manager in the editorial department of a publishing company. Much of the work in your department is done by freelance writers, editors, proofreaders, and page designers who work from home. The editorial manager wants to use the regular freelance staff more effectively. By finding out what sort of hardware and software each one uses, the various types of editorial jobs can be distributed more appropriately between them. The editorial manager asks you to do a short survey of the freelance staff, to see what equipment each one has, and which sorts of jobs they feel they are best equipped to do. The editorial manager also wants to increase the pool of design staff, and asks you to draw up a list freelance designers who might be suitable for the company.

You work out that the job involves:

- analysing the different sorts of editorial jobs, and the equipment and software needed for each;
- investigating freelancer editors' equipment and software;
- drawing up a summary of the sorts of editorial jobs each one is best fitted to do;
- deciding what the company's requirements are for freelance designers;
- finding suitable freelance designers;
- pulling all the information together and writing a report.

You are already very busy doing the sort of work that only you can do, and you feel that this project will take up a lot of time that you could use more effectively.

Which parts of this job would you delegate to someone else, and which would you carry out yourself?

_____

_____

_____

_____

_____

_____

I would suggest that you could delegate to other people in your team:

- the responsibility for analysing the different sorts of jobs, and the equipment and software needed for each;
- surveying freelance editors' equipment and software;
- summarizing the sorts of editorial jobs each one is best fitted to do;
- finding freelance designers who are likely to be short-listed.

You might want to check on the company's requirements for designers before someone else does the work of searching for suitable people. In addition, you will probably want to write the final report, although others might also contribute to it. The final decision about which designers might be interviewed is yours, as is the decision about which editorial jobs best suit which freelance editors.

You may have come up with different answers from these, but they are probably based on similar ideas.

You will probably agree that this project would be a useful opportunity for you to work with your workteam and show them that you have confidence in them. The project is interesting and it also enables you to do some work developing your team members. These factors make parts of the project highly suitable for delegation.

The kinds of jobs which are suitable for delegating may include the following:

- jobs which individual team members can do as well as or better than you;
- jobs which serve to develop individuals;
- jobs which are of low to medium priority;
- jobs which are routine;
- jobs which appeal to individual team members.

Let's look at each of these factors in turn.

3.1 Jobs for which team members are competent

As a team leader you need to concentrate on the management activities of planning, organizing, motivating and controlling your workteam. Although you may like to do some of the technical work you were originally trained for, you should bear in mind that your team members are closer to the actual work than you. Therefore, they are likely to have ready access to the information needed to do the job. So you can delegate the parts of a job, often the technical parts, which another member of the workteam can do just as well as, if not better than, you.

For this kind of job you are building on the **existing competence** of team members, making the most of their existing strengths. Indeed, this is an important way of using delegation.

However, you should also consider delegating tasks which will help team members **develop** competence.

3.2 Developmental jobs

As a team leader you have a responsibility to make sure your team members are skilled and experienced to do the work of the team both now and in the future. You also want to build a team that is well-motivated. For this you need to develop individual team members so that they are able to meet current and future demands. Investing in team members through development activities shows that you value their contribution.

Delegation is a valuable technique here. It allows you to share some of your interesting work, and thus show your trust in your team. It is also an effective way of developing people. The work carried out as part of delegation contributes to the work of the section, so is intrinsically useful. But by the end of the delegation process, the team member should have learned new things which he or she can go on to apply and use.

When you identify jobs that will help develop team members, you need to consider whether you can give them access to the resources necessary to do these jobs properly. Although you can allocate many resources, bear in mind that some – for example, information or particular expertise – cannot always be allocated or made easily accessible.

So consider aspects of your work which may be done by a member of your workteam, who would see them as interesting or challenging, a break in their own routine and an opportunity to develop new skills and experience.

Delegation carried out with these issues in mind can strengthen and empower an individual, because their enthusiasm and commitment have been recognized in a practical way.

3.3 Medium to low priority jobs

Most team leaders have more work to do than they have time for, and so they tend to organize their work according to priority. They focus on jobs which are **urgent** and **important**; in other words high priority jobs. The jobs they leave until last and which may not even get done, are those of lower priority. They may be important, but not urgent, or they may be of relatively low importance. It is these jobs which can be usefully delegated to others.

The chart below shows how jobs may be prioritized according to their importance and urgency, and how far jobs falling into different areas of the chart could be delegated.

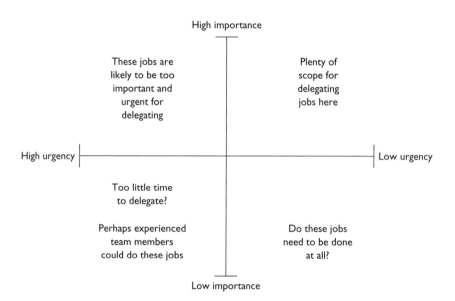

High importance/high urgency   Team leaders are likely to want to do these jobs themselves. The jobs have to be done well and they are needed soon, so there is perhaps not enough time to delegate effectively.

High importance/low urgency   The jobs in this category will become urgent if they are not done now. They are likely to be suitable for delegating as there is time to plan, monitor and review the job. By delegating relatively important jobs, the team leader is demonstrating trust and confidence in the team member. The fact that these jobs are important also suggests that they may be used to develop staff.

Low importance/high urgency   Team leaders may feel that they don't have time to delegate jobs in this category, and that it is quicker to do them themselves. But if team members already have experience in doing these jobs, then the time taken to delegate again will not be great and team leaders can focus on more important work.

Low importance/low urgency   If the job is not important and not urgent, team leaders may question whether the job has to be done at all. However, where jobs still need to be done, they can be effectively delegated to team members.

There are some key advantages in delegating work of lower priority.

- You ensure that these jobs are done.
- You will have time to go through the delegation process thoroughly with jobs that are not urgent. This will be especially necessary when the jobs themselves are important or when you are delegating to an inexperienced team member.
- When you delegate jobs that are of medium to low importance, you will have more time to focus on those which you consider are important.

3.4 Routine jobs

As a team leader you will have responsibility for carrying out a range of routine jobs, for example, monitoring and regular reporting. It makes sense to delegate some of these activities to team members, so that they develop the skills and experience to do these jobs themselves. Delegation here helps to increase team member involvement in the overall work of the section, and can foster appreciation of the purpose and importance of routine activities – which can sometimes seem pointless and time-consuming to team members.

3.5 Attractive jobs

Although not all the tasks that are worth delegating appeal to team members it is worth including some which are generally seen as desirable. Such jobs can be used to reward staff for good performance. Here is an example.

> An international company which has a large workforce based in France regularly sends groups of managers to the UK in order to improve their use of English. They are based at a language school in Bath for two weeks at a time and, although it is a working course, it is also viewed by those who come as a very pleasant trip. Each time a

group comes over, which is about every three months, a member of the company's training department comes with them. Sometimes the head of training comes with the group herself, but often she sends other members of her department instead. Partly this is to improve their own English language, but it is also an example of her willingness to delegate some of the attractive parts of her job.

Activity 24

10 mins

We have looked at some of the kinds of jobs which may be suitable for delegation. Now relate these to your own work. Select two tasks you currently carry out which fit into each of the categories of job listed below. Your tasks can fall into more than one category.

Tasks which team members can do as well as or better than you.

_____

_____

Tasks which serve to develop individuals.

_____

_____

Tasks which are of low to medium priority.

_____

_____

Tasks which are routine.

_____

_____

Tasks which appeal to team members.

_____

_____

The tasks which you have identified may all be suitable for delegation. However, you may also find that those which are most suitable for delegation fall into more than one category. For example, we would argue that a task which is of medium priority and which will also help to develop staff is a prime candidate for delegation.

4 Delegating to volunteers

As a manager, you may well have a responsibility for developing the skills and experience of volunteers. But you can only delegate to volunteers to the extent that they want to accept. With paid employees, you have the last resort of being able to instruct them to do something, but you don't have this option with volunteers. In fact, you have to keep them positively interested and committed all the time or you will lose them. While paid employees may tell you that they are not happy, volunteers are more likely just to stop coming.

It is therefore critically important to share what are seen to be the attractive and sought after tasks equally and fairly. You need to get to know which tasks volunteers regard as attractive. Some volunteers may be keen to acquire new skills and new experiences which will stand them in good stead for paid work in other areas. But you may also find that a particular youth club activity or a shift that fits in well with school hours represent the coveted jobs.

5 Which of your tasks can you delegate?

A work diary is a useful way of finding out the activities we carry out at work.

Activity 25

15 mins

Complete your work diary twice a day over at least three fairly typical working days.

Keep the recording system as simple as possible, so that you really do use it. For example, use a log sheet something like the one shown below.

Name		Date		Sheet Number	
Time		Activity	Type of activity (planning, organizing, motivating, controlling, other)	Duration (min.)	Notes or comments
Started	Finished				

EXTENSION 2
Making a record of all your work activities may be time-consuming, but it is often very revealing – not only for planning delegation, but also for time management. Extension 2 looks at how to use your time wisely.

Many people are surprised when they review their work diaries to discover how they actually spend their time. Many find there is much greater scope for delegation than they first thought.

Activity 26

When you have collected the information about how you spend your time, you then need to analyse it.

First of all separate all the activities which you **need to deal with yourself**. These may be tasks that come under the headings of planning or organizing work and motivating and controlling your workteam, or tasks which your organization requires you to do yourself.

Now put the rest of the tasks under the following headings. They may fall under more than one heading.

Team members competent to do	Developmental	Low to medium priority	Routine	Attractive

You should find that most of the tasks under these headings are suitable for delegation. Circle the ones which you now feel you should have delegated.

Your work in this Activity shows the potential scope for delegating parts of your recent work. You are likely to find that if you had delegated some of your work, you would have had more time to spend on more important tasks.

To decide which of your current tasks you can delegate, you have to work out priorities.

Activity 27

20 mins

S/NVQ B6

This Activity is the first in a series of eleven Activities for which your responses may together form the basis of evidence for your S/NVQ port-folio. If you are intending to take this course of action, it might be better to write your answers on separate sheets of paper.

Make a 'To do' list for the next three to five days. Write down all the things you need to do in the space below.

_____

_____

_____

_____

_____

_____

_____

_____

_____

_____

_____

_____

_____

When you have done this, analyse your list.

Write an 'S' besides those which you feel only you can do.

Write a 'D' next to all those that you immediately feel you can delegate.

EXTENSION 3
Extension 3 deals with
the central problem of
all managers: how to
get the best out of
themselves and their
workteam.

When you have separated those tasks you plan to do yourself and those you can delegate, you should prioritize your tasks by considering how important and how urgent each one is. This will help you to decide the order in which to tackle them, and also to see which of them you could delegate to others.

The way you prioritize tasks depends on your own experience and judgement of what is important. Only you can assess the consequences of not doing the job on time or to the standard needed.

One way of sorting out your priorities is to place each job in the appropriate place on a chart showing scales of importance and urgency, like the one shown earlier (page 50).

Let's see how this works by looking at a case study.

> On Tuesday evening before leaving work, Sandra Wilkinson drew up the following list of tasks which she needed to do the next day. She wrote comments beside each one. The list of tasks was as follows.

Job	Comments
A Arrange farewell presentation	For Thursday lunchtime
B Answer memo from the general manager	Task delegated to me by my boss
C Complete return for the finance department	Already delayed through my having to wait for information
D Prepare information for computer input	Deadline 5 p.m. Friday
E Check suppliers' acceptance of new specification	Should be done before new contract starts
F Prepare unfair dismissal case for industrial tribunal	Must be suitable for my boss to present by Friday
G Write up minutes of team meeting	Promised for Thursday
H Complete report on accident which happened yesterday	Statutory requirement: must complete while fresh in my mind
I Collect/analyse information about results of quality improvement project	Needed for report to my boss by end of month
J Prepare briefing to team on new contract	Briefing meeting Thursday

Sandra first identified those tasks which she felt only she could do. These were: B, F, H and J.

Then she rated the tasks according to their importance and urgency in the following chart.

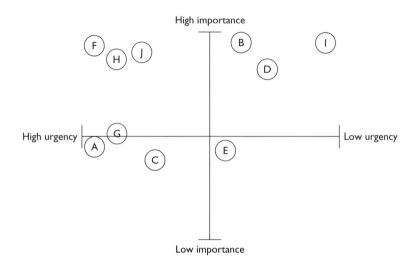

With this information, Sandra decided that in order to get the tasks done she needed to delegate some of her work.

She decided to delegate parts of task A, although she would have to plan what to say. She also felt tasks D, E and I would be developmental tasks which various members of her team would benefit from doing. She decided to ask an experienced team member to write up the team meeting minutes (Task G) – he had done the job once before. Finally, she thought that it would not take her long to complete the return for finance, and she thought that although urgent, she could delay the job until Thursday, if necessary. Of the tasks which she had to do herself, she felt she could delay task B, but the others had to be done on Wednesday.

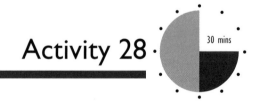

Activity 28

30 mins

S/NVQ
B6

This Activity is the second in a series of eleven Activities for which your responses may together form the basis of evidence for your S/NVQ portfolio. If you are intending to take this course of action, it might be better to write your answers on separate sheets of paper.

This Activity asks you to use the importance/urgency matrix to put your tasks in order of priority.

Make a list of the tasks which you labelled 'D' in Activity 22 and give each one a letter starting from A. We've given you space for up to ten tasks, but you can add more if you choose.

A _____

B _____

C _____

D _____

E _____

F _____

G _____

H _____

I _____

J _____

Now prioritize them by placing them in appropriate positions in the chart below.

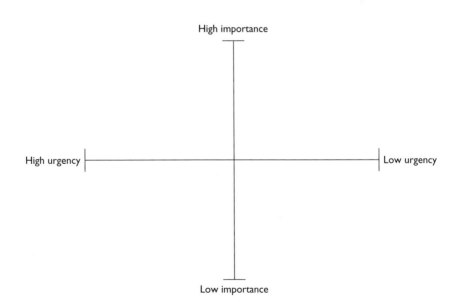

This prioritizing of tasks should show you tasks which you need to carry out yourself and which ones may be suitable for delegating. Now consider which of these tasks:

■ staff are competent to do;

_____

_____

_____

■ are developmental;

_____

_____

_____

■ are routine;

_____

_____

_____

■ are attractive to do.

_____

_____

_____

I hope you have seen that prioritizing your work according to importance and urgency helps you to see where you need to direct your efforts and your opportunities for delegating.

Activity 29

S/NVQ
B6

This Activity is the third in a series of eleven Activities for which your responses may together form the basis of evidence for your S/NVQ portfolio. If you are intending to take this course of action, it might be better to write your answers on separate sheets of paper.

Select a job which you want to delegate to a team member. It may be one of those which you identified in Activity 27 or Activity 28.

As you work through the rest of the workbook you will go through the process of planning and controlling the delegation. So you should choose a job that is reasonably challenging and interesting.

Briefly describe the job here.

_____

_____

_____

Now describe the benefits of delegating this job:

■ to you as team leader;

_____

_____

_____

■ to the person who will be carrying out the delegated task;

_____

_____

_____

■ to the organization.

_____

_____

_____

6 Selecting a team member for delegation

All of your team members can benefit from delegation, and you should look for opportunities to delegate to everyone in your team. But if you have a particular job to delegate, you need to think about who is the 'right' person to do the job.

This involves considering the requirements of the job and the needs of your team members. Let's look at the requirements of the job first.

There are four questions to ask.

- What experience, expertise, skills and attitudes are needed to do the job? The job may require a high level of technical know-how or previous experience, which only certain members of your team possess.
- How urgent is the job? If you need the job done urgently, you will have less time to spend briefing and supporting an inexperienced team member. You may want to delegate an urgent job to someone who has done a similar task before, and who is already competent to do it.
- What are the consequences of missing deadlines, or making mistakes? By thinking about the importance of getting the job right first time and the deadline for completing it, you can judge the level of risk you are prepared to take in giving the task to someone who has never done it before.
- What is the most economical way of getting the job done?

Let's look at an example to explain this last point.

Activity 30

5 mins

Bill Pearce, a team leader of a graphics design shop, was complaining to his boss that he found himself spending a large part of his working day using the photocopying machine.

If you were Bill's manager, how would you recommend Bill overcomes the problem?

_____

_____

_____

_____

You may agree that managers who spend much of their time photocopying materials are not using their time cost effectively. Surely the task could more often be given to somebody whose time represents a lower cost to the organization? The activity shows how particular jobs are often done at a totally uneconomic rate.

Sometimes you may decide it is worth using more resources in delegating a job than absolutely necessary, especially if you plan to use delegation for team development.

This takes us on to thinking about who among the team members is the best person to carry out the job.

We have seen that you may want to delegate tasks to team members who are already competent to carry them out. In this way you are acknowledging and making use of the expertise and skills of team members. However, it is not always appropriate to select the person whose skills and experience are the most suitable for the job.

Delegation is an important technique for developing competence across your team. As a manager you need to be thinking about developing your team members so that they are able to meet the current challenges of their work, and are prepared to meet future challenges. So it may be a good idea to delegate a particular job to someone who needs to learn how to do it as part of a development programme, or to gain further experience in carrying out a task of which he or she already has limited knowledge.

Again there are a number of questions to ask.

■ Who will find the job challenging and/or interesting?
■ Who will benefit from taking on the job?
■ Who has the skills, expertise and attitudes needed to do the job?
■ Who has carried out a similar job before?
■ Who do you think has the necessary skills, but has not yet used them for a job like this?
■ Who could do the job with some coaching or help from another member of the team?
■ Who is available to do the job?
■ Can you reorganize someone's work so that he or she becomes available to take on the job?
■ Is there someone who would regard doing the job as a form of recognition and/or reward?

Bear in mind that delegation can be used as part of training and development.

Activity 31

30 mins

**S/NVQ
D6**

This Activity is the fourth in a series of eleven Activities for which your responses may together form the basis of evidence for your S/NVQ portfolio. If you are intending to take this course of action, it might be better to write your answers on separate sheets of paper.

This Activity helps you to work out the best person to take on the job you have chosen to delegate.

First consider the requirements of the job, and write notes under the headings below.

Skills, expertise and attitudes required.

_____

_____

_____

_____

How urgent the job is.

_____

_____

_____

_____

Consequences of not getting it right.

_____

_____

_____

_____

Most cost-effective way of doing the job.

_____

_____

_____

_____

Now think about your team members by answering the following questions.

Who will find the job challenging and/or interesting?

_____

_____

Who will benefit from taking on the job?

_____

_____

Who has the skills, expertise and attitudes needed to do the job?

_____

_____

Who has carried out a similar job before?

_____

_____

Who has the necessary skills, but has not yet used them for a job like this?

_____

_____

Who could do the job with some coaching or help from another member of the team?

_____

_____

Who is available to do the job?

_____

_____

Can you reorganize someone's work so that he or she becomes available to take on the job?

_____

_____

Is this job suitable as a form of reward or recognition? If so, to whom might it be delegated for this purpose?

_____

_____

In the light of your comments about the job itself and your team members, who is the best person to do the job?

_____

_____

I hope you agree that the systematic approach taken in this activity helps you to take account of all the angles when selecting the most suitable person to carry out a delegated task.

You may find it useful to adopt a similar approach when you are preparing to delegate other tasks.

EXTENSION 4
Extension 4 looks at how to delegate tasks to your team, rather than simply to individuals.

By now you should have chosen a suitable task for delegating and selected the most appropriate person to do the job. You have gone through the stages of preparing for delegation. In the next session you will be carrying out the delegation.

Self-assessment 3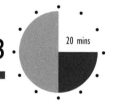

20 mins

Here is a list of tasks which a manager has drawn up.

a See Carole about being late in to work. ☐

b Deal with staff grievance. ☐

c Investigate the problem with no. 2 machine – used by operators. ☐

d Write up minutes of team meeting. ☐

e Organize date, place and time for quality improvement project meeting. ☐

f Brief supplier on new product specification. ☐

g Prepare month's production figures for manager. ☐

h Liaise with training about team's health and safety needs. ☐

1　Tick those which you think may be suitable for delegating.

2　Which ones are definitely unsuitable for delegating and why?

_____

_____

_____

_____

_____

_____

3　Why might you delegate a task to a team member who has not had experience in doing the task?

_____

_____

4　Why might you delegate a task to a team member who has the expertise and experience in doing the task?

_____

_____

_____

Answers to these questions can be found on page 105.

7 Summary

- You cannot delegate all your work. Examples of **work you cannot delegate** include:

  - work of a confidential nature;
  - activities your organization requires you to carry out yourself;
  - work which you do not have the authority to delegate.

- Jobs which you **can delegate** to others include those:

  - which can be done just as well by a member of your workteam;
  - for which a member of your workteam is technically more able, or has easier access to the relevant information;
  - which help to develop team members and which may be interesting and/or challenging;
  - of medium or low priority;
  - which are routine;
  - which are attractive, and may be part of your system of recognition and reward to team members.

- If you **manage volunteers**, you must keep them committed and motivated to do the work. This may mean offering them new experiences and opportunities to develop new skills, but it may also mean getting to know the coveted jobs and allocating them fairly and equally.

- To find the right person to do a job, you need to consider first the **requirements of the job**, and then the **needs of your team members**.

- In considering the requirements of the job, think about the following.

  - The skills and expertise needed to do the job.
  - The importance and urgency of the job.
  - The degree of risk you are able to take.
  - The most cost-effective way of doing the job.

- The right person for the job may be:
  - the person with the necessary skills, expertise and experience;
  - someone who has the skills and expertise, but has not yet had experience in doing the job;
  - someone whose skills you want to develop through delegating;
  - someone who has the time to do the work, or whose workload can be reorganized so they are available to do it;
  - a person whose work and commitment you would like to recognize and/or reward in a practical way.

Session D
Carrying out delegation

You have begun the process of delegating effectively by selecting an appropriate job to delegate and by choosing a member of your workteam to carry it out. In this session you will continue the process by carrying out the delegation. This involves:

- setting clear objectives;
- planning the delegated task;
- monitoring the task when it is being carried out;
- reviewing the results of the delegation with the team member.

You may recall that we introduced the full process in Session A.

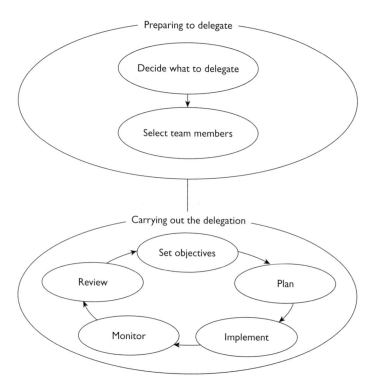

2 Setting objectives

As we saw in Session A, everyone in an organization needs to know their particular objectives – so they know where they are heading. Clear objectives allow everyone to:

■ know precisely what has to be done;
■ judge when it has been achieved.

So when you are delegating you need to write down objectives that the person who is carrying out the task can understand and use.

An effective objective is SMART. This stands for the following.

■ **Specific** – stating exactly what has to be achieved, although not **how** the job should be done.
■ **Measurable** – so that you can tell when the task has been done properly; it might involve a description of the results of the task, or standards for doing the job.
■ **Achievable** – the objective has to be realistic in the circumstances, given the resources that are available, for example, people, equipment, materials, money, information and time, and the people who will carry it out must agree to it.
■ **Relevant** – the objective must be seen as relating both to the job roles of those who are to achieve the objective and to the wider objectives of the organization.
■ **Time bound** – it is important to give some guidance about deadlines and time-frames for achieving the objective, again, these should be realistic.

It should also contribute to the objectives of the team or section.

So in order to write SMART objectives you need to know exactly what it is you want done, what resources will be needed to do the job and when it is to be done.

Activity 32

Imagine you have been given the following set of objectives.

'The job involves finding out about customer complaints in this section.

At the end of this task you will have:

- collected information about customer complaints between April last year and end March this year – using data stored in the customer complaints file in Jackie's office area;
- organized and summarized that information;
- presented findings to the supervisor in a short (3–4 page) report in hard copy and in Word, using tables or charts to summarize the information.'

How SMART are these objectives? What additional information, if any, is needed to make the objectives SMART? Write your ideas below under the following headings.

Specific.

_____

_____

_____

Measurable.

_____

_____

_____

Achievable.

_____

_____

_____

Relevant.

_____

_____

_____

Time bound.

_____

_____

_____

You probably agree that the objectives do not meet the SMART criteria. Although we know the period to be investigated, the objectives do not specify which customer complaints should be examined and they do not state what sort of information is needed. There are no details about how to organize the information, for example, does it need to be organized by type of customer, type of complaint or response to the complaint? We have more details about handing the information to the supervisor, but there is no time guideline, so we don't know when the job has to be completed. There is some indication of resources in the mention of the customer complaints file, and we will need to make sure we will have access to Word on computer in order to write the report. The vague wording of the objectives will make it difficult to know when they have been achieved, although the presentation of the report is one indication.

Before we could agree to these objectives, some important details will have to be sorted out.

To make the objectives SMART they could be refined as follows.

> 'Senior management have asked for a report about how well the customer care policy is working. To do this we need to find out how we have handled all customer complaints over the past year.
>
> Your job is to:
>
> - collect information about all customer complaints between April last year and end March this year – using data stored in the customer complaints file held in Jackie's office area;
> - organize and summarize that information under the following headings:
>   - type of customer;
>   - nature of the complaint;
>   - how the complaint was made;
>   - who handled the complaint;
>   - how the complaint was dealt with;
>   - response times;
>   - present findings to the supervisor in a short (3–4 page) report in hard copy and on disk in the normal program (Word), using tables or charts to summarize the information.
>
> The deadline for this job is 15 May.'

Notice that the objectives here include a brief statement about why it is necessary. While it could be argued that the purpose of a job is not strictly part of the objectives, it certainly helps people if they understand why they are going to do it. Look at the following case.

Rebecca Davis was about to rush off to a meeting with clients, but she had time for a quick word with Steve Gould first. 'Look, I have to go, but I've just heard from the warehouse that the printers have finally delivered the brochures. Can you arrange to have them transferred over here by 2.30 p.m. at the latest?' Steve agreed and Rebecca disappeared out of the room. Steve arranged for the warehouse to interrupt another job and deliver the 10,000 brochures to reception by 2.00 p.m. At 2.40 p.m. Rebecca came out of her meeting and found Steve. 'Where are the brochures?' Steve explained that they were all down in reception. Rebecca pulled a face. 'But I only need two or three of them to show to the clients.'

Just a simple misunderstanding, perhaps. But if Rebecca had explained **why** she needed the brochures, then she would have saved herself some embarrassment, and she would have saved Steve and the warehouse some valuable time.

Activity 33

S/NVQ
D6

This Activity is the fifth in a series of eleven Activities for which your responses may together form the basis of evidence for your S/NVQ portfolio. If you are intending to take this course of action, it might be better to write your answers on separate sheets of paper.

Think about what is involved in carrying out the task you are planning to delegate. Think about what the team member who will be doing the work will require to complete the task successfully.

When you have considered these aspects, write SMART objectives for the task you are planning to delegate. Make sure that these objectives link up with the wider objectives of your team or section.

_____

_____

_____

_____

_____

_____

_____

_____

_____

_____

Check whether your objectives are linked to the work of your team and that they are:

- specific – so that the task is clearly defined and explained;
- measurable – so that the team member can tell when he or she has successfully achieved the task;
- achievable – the resources required are available;
- relevant – everyone involved is clear why they're being asked to do the task;
- time bound – there is a clear deadline for completion of the task.

Be prepared to improve your objectives. You may find it helpful to put yourself in the shoes of the person to whom you will be delegating. Will the team member understand exactly what is required in doing the job when he or she reads them?

3 Planning

When you have set the objectives you need to give further consideration to the task you are delegating and then discuss it with the team member. In this section we look at:

- planning resources;
- briefing the team member.

3.1 Planning resources

When you are delegating you need to give the team member the necessary authority and resources to carry out the task.

Consider how you will make sure that the team member has the necessary authority to carry out the task, particularly where this involves other people. You may have to inform others that the team member will be acting on your behalf. Other people are just one of the resources that may be required to do the job. How will you make sure that the resources needed are available? For example, do you need to give the team member a budget to work with?

Activity 34

15 mins

S/NVQ D6

This Activity is the sixth in a series of eleven Activities for which your responses may together form the basis of evidence for your S/NVQ portfolio. If you are intending to take this course of action, it might be better to write your answers on separate sheets of paper.

In Activity 33 you developed objectives for the task you are planning to delegate.

Now consider the resources you need to allocate to your team member. Make a note of these resources in the left-hand column. In the right-hand column write any action you need to take to make sure these resources are available.

Resources needed	How to make them available

You may have considered the following resources:

- people;
- machinery and equipment;
- materials;
- finance;
- information;
- time.

As we have seen, you keep overall responsibility for the task you are delegating, so it is up to you to make sure the task is completed successfully and all the objectives are achieved. Plan to monitor the important parts of the job while it is underway. You may want to monitor the use of resources, as well as the way the job is done.

You should also plan to review it when it is completed. Consider suitable rewards for work that is done well. These can be of many different forms, such as praise, greater work independence, or maybe something tangible, such as a bonus or promotion.

We will look at monitoring and reviewing in more detail later in this session, but you do have to think about these aspects while you are planning.

3.2 Briefing the team member

EXTENSION 1
Extension 1 looks at effective communications and at making the most of meetings.

Briefing the team member about the task is an opportunity to refine the plan and amend it where necessary.

Bear in mind that you are not simply informing a team member about the task. You want to give this person responsibility to do the job so you want to gain their interest, involvement and commitment. The aim of the discussion is to reach agreement on all aspects of the task.

Look on the briefing as an opportunity to **consult** rather than simply to **inform**.

The best way of doing this is to ask them for their views, and to be prepared to modify your ideas in the light of their contribution. Use the briefing as an opportunity to develop the plan with the team member. Remember that the team member is going to carry out the work, so they need to be comfortable with it.

Here is a suggested approach to briefing.

- Explain the task and what you want to achieve. You may want to explain that you see it as a development opportunity for the team member, or that you are delegating the job to the team member because you know they have the skills, experience and expertise to do a good job.

- Ask the team member to tell you how they would do the job, rather than instructing them how to do it. In this way you will get a clear idea about the team member's approach and can judge whether your plan for controlling the job is pitched at the right level.
- Ask the team member to decide what resources they think they will need to meet the objectives for the job, including any help they will need from you. Then discuss your views on resources and how you will make them available.
- Ask the team member to estimate the time it is likely to take. Then discuss with them your views on the timing, interim deadlines and so on.
- Agree how you will keep track of progress and offer support and guidance, so that the team member can come to you to discuss any ideas or problems they have.

It is important to give the team member enough time to reflect and consider how they will do the job. Bear in mind that although you are familiar with the task, it is all new to the team member. You may need to schedule a follow-up meeting so the team member can come back to you with their thoughts and suggestions on how they will carry out the job.

Activity 35

**S/NVQs
B6, D6**

This Activity is the seventh in a series of eleven Activities for which your responses may together form the basis of evidence for your S/NVQ portfolio. If you are intending to take this course of action, it might be better to write your answers on separate sheets of paper.

Write out a checklist or briefing document for delegating on which both you and the team member can record the agreed details of the task. The document should cover all the areas you need to consider when discussing the task with the team member.

Check that your document includes headings and space for the following information.

- The purpose of the task.
- The objectives.
- The resources available.
- The support available.
- How to monitor the task and keep track of progress.
- When and how you will review the task.

Activity 36

20 mins

S/NVQs
B6, D6

This Activity is the eighth in a series of eleven Activities for which your responses may together form the basis of evidence for your S/NVQ portfolio. If you are intending to take this course of action, it might be better to write your answers on separate sheets of paper.

Use your checklist to brief your team member on the task you have chosen to delegate.

Now make brief notes on how well the briefing went by answering the following questions.

How well did you describe the background and purpose of the job?

_____

_____

_____

How did you explain why you have selected the team member to do the job?

_____

_____

_____

How well did you talk through with the team member:

■ the objectives?

_____

■ the resource requirements?

_____

■ how you and others can provide support?

_____

■ how to monitor progress?

_____

■ how to review the task?

_____

What contributions did the team member make to the discussion?

_____

_____

_____

_____

How would you describe the team member's attitude towards the task? (Committed, enthusiastic, confident, apprehensive?)

_____

_____

_____

_____

How successful was the briefing?

_____

_____

_____

What will you do next time to improve the briefing?

_____

_____

_____

A successful briefing depends on good planning and effective communication on the part of the manager. This means listening carefully, responding appropriately and checking understanding. Remember that a successful briefing will lead to agreement about the task. You will feel confident that the job you have delegated is in good hands, and that the team member knows what to do, how to do it, by when and with what results. You will also feel that the team member is committed to doing the job well.

After the briefing the team member should begin to carry out the job. Although you have handed over the job you will still need to check on progress through monitoring.

4 Monitoring the delegated task

By monitoring a job, you stay in control, you will be able to see potential problems at an early stage and you can guide your team member to make any necessary changes to keep the job on course.

Remember that the level of direct control you have over a job is related to the amount of trust you have in the team member doing a good job. Bear in mind how the team member is likely to respond if you show little confidence in their abilities and keep intervening in the job. Whenever you delegate, you are taking some risk, because you are sharing your responsibility for the job with another person.

The key to monitoring work that you delegate is to agree the following with the team member at the start.

- Objectives – what you want to achieve.
- Time scales and deadlines – what aspects of the job need to be completed by when.
- Critical activities – the key parts of a job, on which the success of the whole job depends.

You can then agree to monitor the job against these benchmarks. There are many ways of monitoring, as shown below.

- Having informal discussions with a team member when you meet him or her on-the-job.
- Collecting information, such as operating temperatures of machinery, attendance records, numbers of telephone calls made, number of client contacts made.
- Arranging to review progress with the team member perhaps by a report or an informal meeting. Progress reviews may be planned in advance and determined by time, stages in the job or other factors.
- Agreeing with a team member that they will come to you if they predict any problems or difficulties in getting the job done as previously agreed.
- Examining the results of work – a manufactured product, a report, etc.
- Observing a team member carrying out some aspect of the job, a discussion with a customer or colleague, for example.

Team members are usually actively involved in collecting, recording and communicating information for monitoring. Although this information may come to you so that you can keep overall control of the work, team members themselves often know when the work is going well and when a job is going off-course. They can usually suggest solutions, if encouraged to do so.

By getting team members to monitor aspects of a task themselves, you are giving them scope to control the work, to take appropriate action if they foresee any problems. This shows that you trust them.

If you uncover a potential problem while monitoring the delegated task, be tactful in pointing it out to the team member, for example, choose a quiet place where you won't be overheard. Encourage the team member to offer solutions. Bear in mind that your aim is to support the team member and help him or her be successful.

Activity 37

This Activity is the ninth in a series of eleven Activities for which your responses may together form the basis of evidence for your S/NVQ portfolio. If you are intending to take this course of action, it might be better to write your answers on separate sheets of paper.

What methods are you using to monitor the job you have delegated?

_____

_____

_____

How involved is the team member in monitoring?

_____

_____

_____

Think about the level of direct control you have over the task, and the level of trust this shows that you have in your team member.

Mark the spectrum below to indicate your level of control and trust.

high control	low control
low trust	high trust

It is worth thinking about whether you have chosen an appropriate level of control and trust. You can do this when you come to review the delegated task.

● 5 Reviewing the delegation

Although you may review progress while the job is underway, you will want to carry out a thorough review soon after a delegated task has been completed. It is an important opportunity for you and your team member to consider the success – or otherwise – of the task, to learn from the experience and plan improvements for the future.

Your review may cover different aspects of the task, including the process of delegating. For example, you may want to look at:

- the extent to which the objectives have been met or have had to be changed;
- the use made of resources;
- the effectiveness of support given to the team member;
- how well the task was monitored and controlled;
- any difficulties or problems;
- the team member's performance in carrying out the job and how he or she can build on what has been learned.

When reviewing a delegated task, it is best to let your team member get the praise for work successfully done, but to accept the blame yourself when things have gone wrong. The reason for this is that you have to accept overall responsibility, including the decision to delegate in the first place.

An important part of any review will be the feedback that you give to the team member on their performance.

Activity 38 · 5 mins

Note down what you think is the purpose of giving feedback to a team member about their performance in carrying out a delegated task.

_____

_____

_____

_____

I hope you agree that the aim of giving feedback is to help the team member learn from the experience – both the successes and failures – so that they can do better next time. It is the key to encouraging staff to develop, so it is an important part of your responsibilities as a manager.

Feedback should be designed to improve performance.

As a team leader you will probably give informal feedback to team members frequently, but it is also important to set aside some time to have a one-to-one meeting with the team member to give formal feedback.

Giving feedback on good performance does not usually represent a problem – as long as you **still** do give feedback. Successful people need as much development as unsuccessful ones. Feedback on good performance should encourage team members to reflect, identify what has contributed to their success, and consider what they would do differently next time.

When we have to point out mistakes and poor performance we have to work hard to avoid criticizing. Think about how you react when someone criticizes you. Most people agree that if they feel they are being criticized, they get upset or resentful, make excuses or stop listening.

If feedback makes someone feel bad or useless, then it has not served its purpose. Even if you have to point out mistakes, it is important that what you say is encouraging and designed to increase motivation.

Here are eight simple guidelines for giving effective feedback.

1 **Never give feedback when you are angry or frustrated**. You need to be calm, thinking about solving any problem and moving forward.

2 **Give praise where it is due**. It is all too easy to forget the aspects of a job that have been done well, especially when there are other problems. Be specific in your praise, highlighting those aspects of a job that were handled well, or where the team member showed good judgement.

3 **Encourage the person to whom you are giving feedback to contribute their ideas**. These might include what they think they did well, what went wrong and why, and how they would do things next time. By getting the person to assess their own performance you will have a clear idea of areas of agreement, and areas where you need to give more guidance about mistakes.

4 **Be specific about mistakes**. Give exact instances so that the other person can recognize where mistakes were made.

5 **Criticize the action or the behaviour, not the person**. For example, don't say, 'You were wrong to …', instead say that a particular action was wrong.

6 **Investigate the cause of any difficulty**. Was it an instance of bad judgement, was it to do with lack of resources, was it owing to lack of support from you?

7 **Offer support**. How can you help the person solve the problem for the future? Does the person need training? Do they need more support from you or from a team member?

8 **End on a positive note by looking forward to making improvements next time around**. Looking ahead enables both you and the person to whom you are giving feedback to put any mistakes of the past to rest, and move forward.

This kind of feedback is an important aspect of your responsibilities for the development of staff. It doesn't cost anything, except your time, but it's this kind of attention which can make a real difference to people's careers and commitment.

Activity 39

S/NVQs B6, D6

This Activity is the tenth in a series of eleven Activities for which your responses may together form the basis of evidence for your S/NVQ portfolio. If you are intending to take this course of action, it might be better to write your answers on separate sheets of paper.

Plan a feedback session with your team member to review his or her performance in carrying out the delegated task.

When is the review session?

_____

What did the team member do well?

_____

_____

_____

_____

What mistakes were made?

_____

_____

_____

_____

Why do **you** think mistakes were made?

_____

_____

_____

_____

What suggestions do you have for making improvements in the future?

_____

_____

_____

_____

What are the next steps for the team member, for instance, more responsibility and involvement in the team, some coaching, a training course?

_____

_____

_____

_____

You may ask the team member to plan for the session in a similar way, by considering what went well, where improvements could be made next time and so on. Your team member's self-assessment is important, and you could use it as evidence in your portfolio.

Use your plan to carry out the feedback session. Then assess how well it went in the next activity.

Activity 40

20 mins

S/NVQ B6

This Activity is the last in a series of eleven Activities for which your responses may together form the basis of evidence for your S/NVQ portfolio. If you are intending to take this course of action, it might be better to write your answers on separate sheets of paper.

Assess your feedback session by answering the following questions.

What aspects of the feedback session went well? Why?

_____

_____

_____

_____

What aspects of the session could have gone better? Why?

_____

_____

_____

_____

What contribution did the team member make to the session?

_____

_____

_____

_____

How did the team member feel about the feedback you gave? For example, were you able to agree about his or her performance? Did you agree on the next steps?

_____

_____

_____

_____

What will you do differently the next time you give feedback?

_____

_____

_____

_____

Giving constructive feedback is not easy, and it takes practice to give feedback which helps team members improve performance. If you have identified areas for improvement, you are working towards developing your feedback skills.

To delegate effectively you need to use a range of management skills: planning, organizing, communicating, briefing, supporting, controlling and giving feedback.

Delegating will give you more time to concentrate on your important work, but, more significantly perhaps, by using the process of delegating and delegating effectively, you will also develop your team and your relationship of trust with team members.

Self-assessment 4 ·

10 mins

1 Describe the features of a SMART objective.

S _____

M _____

A _____

R _____

T _____

For questions 2 to 5, complete the sentences with a suitable word or words.

2 When briefing a team member make sure that you and they _____ all aspects of the task.

3 _____ involves collecting information about how well a task is going, and enables you or the team member to take action to prevent problems from becoming serious.

4 After the delegated task has been done, you should _____ its successes and failures, so that you can make improvements next time.

5 Part of a review involves giving _____ to the team member on his or her performance.

6 Complete the eight guidelines for giving constructive feedback listed below.

a Never give feedback when you are _____.

b Give _____ where it is due.

c Encourage the person to whom you are giving feedback to _____.

d Be specific about _____.

e Criticize the _____, not the person.

f Investigate the _____ of any difficulty.

g Offer _____.

h End on _____.

Answers to these questions can be found on page 105.

6 Summary

- **Objectives** state what you want to achieve.

- Objectives should be **SMART**.

  - Specific.
  - Measurable.
  - Achievable.
  - Relevant.
  - Time bound.

- When planning the delegation, make sure that:

  - the necessary **authority** for carrying out the task is given;
  - the necessary **resources** are made available.

- The purpose of **briefing** a team member when delegating to them is to reach agreement about all aspects of the task, including the objectives and to gain their **commitment** to do the task.

- When discussing the task **ask the team member** how they would do it, what resources they think they would need, and so on, and then discuss your views.

- **Monitoring** enables you to keep track of progress and take action to keep a job on course if there are problems.

- You can use formal and informal methods to monitor a delegated task and encourage team members to take part in monitoring.

- Make sure you are available to offer **support** to the team member when needed.

- Your **review** of the delegation when the task is completed should include giving **feedback** on the team member's performance.

- Giving feedback is an important part of your responsibility to develop staff.

- Give feedback sensitively in order to help the team member improve his or her performance in the future.

Performance checks

1 Quick quiz

Question 1   What three issues should you consider in allocating work to your team?

_____

_____

Question 2   Outline the five stages in allocating work to people.

_____

_____

_____

Question 3   What does delegation mean?

_____

_____

Question 4   Briefly explain how delegation can improve decision making.

_____

_____

Question 5   How do you keep overall responsibility for a job which you have delegated?

_____

_____

Question 6   Describe the stages in the process of effective delegation.

_____

_____

_____

_____

_____

_____

_____

_____

_____

_____

Question 7   How can you use delegation to develop trust in your team?

_____

_____

Question 8   Give one key advantage to you – as a team leader – of delegating.

_____

_____

Question 9   What improvements in team or individual performance are likely to result from effective delegation?

_____

_____

Question 10   Which tasks ought you to delegate?

_____

_____

_____

_____

Question 11   Can you delegate your responsibility for health and safety?

_____

Question 12   Why do you need to set objectives for a task you are delegating?

_____

_____

_____

Question 13   What resources might need to be allocated to a team member when you are delegating?

_____

_____

_____

Question 14   What are you seeking to achieve when briefing a team member about a delegated task?

_____

_____

_____

Question 15   Why do you need to monitor a delegated task?

_____

_____

Question 16   What is the aim of giving feedback?

_____

_____

Answers to these questions can be found on page 107.

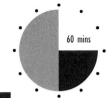

60 mins

2 Workbook assessment

Read the following case study and then answer the questions which follow, writing your answers on a separate sheet of paper.

Charlie Scrimshaw is the head of the contracts department of a large advertising agency. He started work with the company originally as a member of the sales team, and is much happier when talking to people rather than sitting behind a desk. As a result of this preference, his paperwork is seldom up to date.

The business is passing through a period of rapid expansion and, as a result of this, a number of new members have been added to Charlie's team, bringing the total for whom he is responsible to thirty-five. Unfortunately, as control systems are not something with which Charlie is familiar, he has tended to try to get along without them. One result of this is that he doesn't plan very far ahead. He says he cannot find time for planning, as he has too much to do which is concerned with current work. Other members of his department have been heard to describe his management approach as 'lurching from one immediate crisis to the next'.

Charlie believes in what he refers to as an 'open door' policy of managing, making himself always available to members of his workteam whenever they go to his office. He regards this as an important part of his team building, but unfortunately it results in his being constantly interrupted, often for rather trivial reasons. Charlie does not believe in spending a lot of time over making decisions; rather, he regards himself as a 'man of action'. Sometimes, however, his first decision proves to be not very suitable and so after consulting with others, he often quickly changes his mind. A few of Charlie's team members were discussing his method of making decisions during their coffee break the other day. One of them described him as coming to conclusions 'with his mind uncluttered with facts', whilst another said that getting decisions from him was rather like making an instant cup of coffee, 'just add water and stir'.

As a group, they generally agreed that he was a nice guy and a good salesman, but they were concerned that he seemed to spend little time making sure that targets were likely to be met, and only took notice when things had already gone badly astray.

1   What do you think ought to be done at a higher level in the company in order to assist Charlie generally with his supervisory problems?

2   Suggest how Charlie could find the time in which to carry out some forward planning.

3   What can Charlie do to change from his crisis management to being more in control of things?

4   How could Charlie prevent himself being interrupted by his team unnecessarily, but still maintain a good working relationship with them?

5   If you were Charlie, what would you do to make sure you were aware of approaching target dates in time to take any necessary corrective action?

Your complete answer to this assessment need not be longer than a single page.

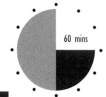

3 Work-based assignment

S/NVQs B6, D6

The time guide for this assignment gives you an approximate idea of how long it is likely to take you to write up your findings. You will need to spend some additional time gathering information, perhaps talking to colleagues and thinking about the assignment and planning.

Your work on this assignment can form part of your evidence for your S/NVQ portfolio.

For this assignment, you are asked to plan a task which you want to delegate in the light of what you have learned in this workbook. There are three stages to this assignment.

1   Identify which of your jobs in the near future you can delegate.

   ■ List the jobs you will need to do over the next few days to a week.
   ■ Put a 'D' beside those which you can delegate.
   ■ For the rest, put them in an order of priority, using the importance/urgency matrix, and identify those which could be done by other members of your team.
   ■ Now choose one of your 'to be delegated' tasks to plan for this assignment. Write brief notes to explain why you have chosen this task.

2 Select an appropriate member of your team to carry out the task. Consider the needs of the task and the needs of your team members. You may find it useful to complete a form like the one in Activity 31. Explain the thinking behind your decision.

3 When you have selected the right person to do the job, you should begin to plan it – the third stage.

Explain how you intend to conduct the briefing. Then draw up notes to help you to explain the task to the team member. The notes should include:

■ suitable objectives for the task;
■ what resources you feel will be needed and how they are to be made available;
■ how the team member can get support and help in doing the task;
■ how the task will be monitored – your role and the role of the team member;
■ when and how the task will be reviewed, and what aspects of the task will be reviewed.

You could use the briefing document you drew up in Activity 30 to help you plan the briefing.

Your completed assignment should contain:

■ lists and charts showing your jobs, and how you prioritized them, together with an explanation of the 'to be delegated' job which you have selected to plan for this assignment;
■ a systematic explanation of why you have selected a particular person from your team to carry out the delegation: you could use the questions in Activity 31 to make sure you explore all the issues;
■ a briefing document and a paragraph or two explaining your intended approach to the briefing.

In all, this assignment does not have to be more than three or four pages long.

You can also take your work on this assignment further, by collecting evidence as the delegated task is carried out. For example, you could review how well the briefing session went, show how the task is monitored and how you and the team member reviewed the task. Bear in mind that the team member who carries out the delegation can contribute appropriate evidence, such as an assessment of how he or she fared.

Reflect and review

1 Reflect and review

Now that you have completed your work on *Organizing and Delegating;* let us review the workbook objectives. The first objective is:

- plan and allocate work to your team.

  In the first session we looked at the primary responsibility of first line managers, to make sure that the teams they manage do their work efficiently and effectively.

- Do you understand how demand for the products or services you supply varies, and what impact this has on the work that your team has to perform?
- Do you ensure that the people you manage are making the best use of their skills to do the tasks that are required?
- Can you identify how future changes in the work that your team does and their productivity will affect the number of people you will need, and their skills?

  The next objective is:

- you should be better able to explain why delegation is an important management technique.

  In Session B we looked at the meaning of delegation and defined some of the terms we would be using. We explored the importance of delegating, and the advantages to you as a team leader of delegating work.

- Have you identified some ways in which delegation can help you, your team members and your organization?

- Have you thought of discussing with your manager and your workteam how you could delegate more effectively to everyone's benefit?

The next objective is:

- You should be better able to use the process of delegation to delegate effectively.

In Session B we gave an overview of the process of delegating effectively. The first part of the process was about preparing by:

- selecting an appropriate task, and
- choosing the right person to carry out the task.

The second part of the process is to carry out the delegation by:

- setting objectives;
- planning;
- implementing;
- monitoring;
- reviewing.

By going through this process you will be more able to retain control of the delegated task and make the most of the benefits of delegation. In Sessions C and D we took you through the delegation process in some detail, and enabled you to put delegation into practice in your workplace.

- Consider the example of delegation that you prepared for and carried out as part of your work in this workbook.

- How far has the systematic process of delegation helped you develop your skills as an effective delegator?

- What improvements have you noticed in the way you now delegate? Would your workteam agree with this self-assessment?

If you feel that the process of delegation will help you to manage effectively, then you have achieved the following objective.

- You should be able to control your workteam more efficiently.

Although some people fear that delegation means that you have to give up control, we've seen that effective delegation – through the process we have described – can actually help you to control your team more efficiently.

- How do you feel delegation will help you control your workteam?

If you understand how delegation can help to keep you in control of your team, then you have achieved this final objective.

2 Action plan

Use this plan to further develop for yourself a course of action you want to take. Make a note in the left-hand column of the issues or problems you want to tackle, and then decide what you intend to do, and make a note in column 2.

The resources you need might include time, materials, information or money. You may need to negotiate for some of them, but they could be something easily acquired, like half an hour of somebody's time, or a chapter of a book. Put whatever you need in column 3. No plan means anything without a timescale, so put a realistic target completion date in column 4.

Finally, describe the outcome you want to achieve as a result of this plan, whether it is for your own benefit or advancement, or a more efficient way of doing things.

Desired outcomes			
1 Issues	2 Action	3 Resources	4 Target completion

Actual outcomes

3 Extensions

Extension 1

Book	*Management*
Author	Roger Oldcorn
Edition	Third edition, 1996
Publisher	Pan Books (Business Masters Series), an imprint of Macmillan General Books

Extension 2

Video	*The Unorganised Manager*, Parts 1, 2 and 3
Produced	1983
Publisher	Video Arts Ltd

The first two parts of *The Unorganised Manager* series show that no matter how efficient managers may think they are, they cannot be fully effective until they learn how to manage their time.

In **Part 1: Damnation** a hard-working manager is so disorganized that he unwittingly makes the lives of his family and colleagues a misery. His disorganization leads to an early heart attack and a confrontation with St Peter. By being given a second chance on Earth, he is able to learn the principles of time management in a way that viewers, many of whom will be unaware of their own faults, can easily relate to.

In **Part 2: Salvation** the manager has returned to Earth full of enthusiasm, but his inability to establish priorities and to delegate effectively lands him back in front of St Peter. The programme shows why managers should consider the actual purpose of their jobs, and not the function. They must learn how to schedule time for active tasks, while leaving time for reactive tasks. By delegating and retaining responsibility, they will make more effective use of their own time and that of their team, and contribute to everyone's motivation and morale.

Part 3: Divine Intervention picks up the story in the first two parts of the series but can be used as a stand-alone resource. It shows how effective managers can create time to focus on their teams.

The now organized manager is called to St Peter, this time following an annual health check. Here he learns that his management style still leaves a lot to be desired, since he is failing to organize his team. Through highly memorable wrong-way, right-way scenarios, viewers will learn three steps to successful delegation.

It is the manager's role to ensure that each team member understands their purpose. The manager must define and identify their overall objective and their key result areas so that they know what is expected of them.

Individuals should be set standards to achieve, measurable either by quality, quantity or cost, so that both they and the manager know how they are doing.

And managers must agree targets with individual team members in order to help them develop and realize their potential, or to bring their performance back on track. Following the three steps, the manager will be able to improve the performance and results of individuals, the team and the organization.

Extension 3	Book	*Essential Managers: How to Delegate*
	Author	Robert Heller
	Edition	1998
	Publisher	Dorling Kindersley Essential Managers series

Extension 4	Book	*Leadership Skills*
	Author	John Adair
	Edition	November 1998
	Publisher	Chartered Institute of Personnel and Development (CIPD)

These extensions can be taken up via your ILM Centre. They will either have them or will arrange that you have access to them. However, it may be more convenient to check out the materials with your personnel or training people at work – they may well give you access. There are other good reasons for approaching your own people; for example, they will become aware of your interest and you can involve them in your development.

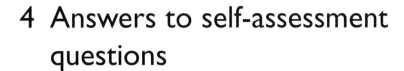
4 Answers to self-assessment questions

Self-assessment 1 on page 18

1 Changes in the level of demand or output of products or services over time are caused by upward or downward TRENDS, SEASONAL variations and UNANTICIPATED variations.

2 In determining what your team is capable of doing, in terms of workload, you need to take account of THE RESOURCES USED, the way that PEOPLE ARE EMPLOYED and their SKILLS.

3 The five stages in allocating work to people are:

1. Break down the team's or department's work objectives into specific targets, tasks or activities.
2. Rank these tasks in terms of priority, based on their *precedence, urgency* and *importance*.
3. Analyse the skills needed for completion of each task.
4. List the skills of the team members.
5. Match people to the tasks.

4 The number of employees needed in future can be calculated by the formula:

$$\frac{\textit{Future work levels}}{\textit{Future labour productivity}}$$

5 The number of people you will need to recruit or make redundant at a future point in time can be calculated by the formula:

Number of employees needed – (Current labour force – Forecast number leaving)

6 The atmosphere is usually reflected in the interactions and communication between people, what standards are set and followed, and to what extent people help and support each other. You may have mentioned other points.

7
- Controlling work effectively is not only a matter of ORGANIZING and employing specific TECHNIQUES – it is also about getting the team to WANT to achieve objectives and to MEASURE up to high standards.
- The better the ATMOSPHERE, and the greater the UNDERSTANDING between team members, the more likely it is that work will be successful and under CONTROL.
- Job ENRICHMENT is one, very significant, approach to MOTIVATION and increased PRODUCTIVITY.
- TRAINING can give the workteam the chance to DEVELOP and broaden its SKILL base.
- The key to controlling work is in managing and MOTIVATING the people.

Self-assessment 2 on page 41

1 Delegation means giving someone **RESPONSIBILITY** and **AUTHOR-ITY** to act on your behalf.

2 If a task is delegated to you, you also need **RESOURCES** allocated to you in order to carry it out.

3 When you delegate a task, you have **OVERALL RESPONSIBILITY** for seeing that a job is done properly and on time.

4 Successful delegation helps to develop team members who are **COMPE-TENT, INVOLVED, COMMITTED** and **WELL-INFORMED**.

5 Delegation enables team leaders to draw on the expertise of team members and so improve **DECISION MAKING**.

6 Time spent delegating is time well spent because:

- it involves developing the competence of team members; this is an important management responsibility;
- it enables you to pass on low to medium priority jobs to others and so concentrate your efforts on high priority work.

7 The term 'span of control' describes the number of people a supervisor is responsible for.

8 Here is the completed diagram:

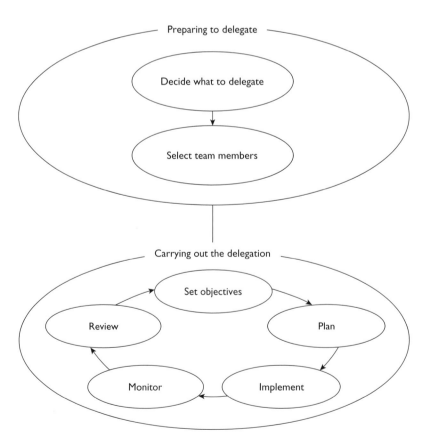

9 The level of **CONTROL** you decide to take when you delegate is related to how much you **TRUST** the person to do a good job.

10 You can develop trust by going through the process of delegation, and helping the team member to be successful by using a high level of control at first.

Self-assessment 3 on page 66

1 I would argue that tasks c, d, e could definitely be delegated. You might also delegate task f.

2 Tasks a and b are definitely not suitable for delegation. Managers have responsibility for their team members' performance, and a manager's concern about lateness cannot be delegated to another member of the team. Organizations' staff grievance procedures usually specify the involvement of the manager in the first instance.

I would also argue that task g is not suitable for delegation, as your manager will expect you to do the job. However, you might want to involve team members in collecting and organizing the information.

Similarly, task h is not suitable, as you are discussing the needs of the whole of your team.

3 You might delegate a task to a team member who has not had experience in doing the task as a way of developing the team member's abilities.

4 You might delegate a task to a team member who has the expertise and experience in doing the task because the task needs to be done well, with few risks of mistakes. It may also be because you or other team members cannot offer much support for doing the job, or because you will not have time to take much direct control over the job.

Self-assessment 4 on page 88

1 A SMART objective is:

- specific;
- measurable;
- achievable;
- relevant;
- time bound.

2 When briefing a team member make sure that you and they **AGREE** all aspects of the task.

3 **MONITORING** involves collecting information about how well a task is going, and enables you or the team member to take action to prevent problems from becoming serious.

4 After the delegated task has been done, you should **REVIEW** its successes and failures, so that you can make improvements next time.

5 Part of a review involves giving **FEEDBACK** to the team member on his or her performance.

6 Here are the eight guidelines to follow.

a Never give feedback when you are ANGRY. You need to be calm, thinking about solving any problem and moving forward.

b Give PRAISE where it is due.

c Encourage the person to whom you are giving feedback to CONTRIBUTE THEIR IDEAS.

d Be specific about MISTAKES.

e Criticize THE ACTION OR THE BEHAVIOUR, not the person.

f Investigate the CAUSE of any difficulty.

g Offer SUPPORT IN SOLVING THE PROBLEM.

h End on a POSITIVE NOTE by looking forward to making improvements next time around.

▪ 5 Answer to Activity 6

1.
$$\frac{\text{Future work levels} = 7{,}500}{\text{Future labour productivity} = 300} = 25 \text{ employees needed}$$

2. 25 employees needed − (32 current labour force − 9* forecast number leaving)

= 25 − 23

= 2 people needed

* 3 will retire, and three will leave in each of the two years.

6 Answers to the quick quiz

Answer 1   In allocating work you need to take account of the resources used, the way that people are employed and their skills.

Answer 2   The five stages in allocating work to people are:

1. Break down the team's or department's work objectives into specific targets, tasks or activities.
2. Rank these tasks in terms of priority, based on their *precedence, urgency* and *importance*.
3. Analyse the skills needed for completion of each task.
4. List the skills of the team members.
5. Match people to the tasks.

Answer 3   Delegation means giving someone the **authority** and the **responsibility** to act on your behalf.

Answer 4   Delegation improves decision making as it draws on the expertise of team members, who are actually carrying out the work of the section.

Answer 5   Team leaders keep overall responsibility for the work which they delegate by going through the process of delegation, and so retaining overall control of the job.

Answer 6   The process of effective delegation can be summarized as follows.

- Prepare for delegating by deciding:
    - what tasks can be delegated;
    - to whom.
- Carry out the delegation by:
    - setting and agreeing the objectives;
    - planning;
    - letting the team member carry out the task;
    - monitoring;
    - reviewing.

Answer 7   You can develop trust in your team by using high levels of control at first, in order to help the team member be successful, and then gradually using lower levels of control as your confidence and trust increase.

Answer 8   There are many possibilities here, depending on how you feel delegation will benefit you. For example, you may feel that a major benefit will be to give you more time to concentrate on your important work, help you to develop your staff or to develop your relationship with team members.

Answer 9   Delegation is a way of developing individuals in your team, improving their competence and skills. Besides this, delegation should help individuals feel well-informed, committed and involved.

Answer 10   There will be tasks which you **have** to do yourself but, of the other tasks you do, you should delegate those that:

- your team members are competent to do;
- will help to develop team members;
- are of medium or low priority;
- are routine;
- are attractive to team members.

Answer 11   No. There are aspects of your work and responsibilities that you cannot delegate. Your own responsibility for health and safety is one of them. Your organization's policies and procedures may suggest others.

Answer 12   Someone who is delegated to do a task has to know what they will be working to achieve and by when. SMART objectives make this quite clear.

Answer 13   Resources include materials, equipment, money, people, time and information.

Answer 14   The briefing should seek to encourage a team member to feel committed and enthusiastic about the task. In the briefing you are seeking to reach agreement about the delegated task.

Answer 15   Monitoring allows you – and the person carrying out the task – to keep an eye on progress, to see where there might be potential problems, and to take corrective action, where appropriate, so that the task meets its objectives.

Answer 16   The purpose of giving feedback is to improve performance. This means that feedback should be given in such a way so as to encourage and motivate a team member.

■ 7 Certificate

Completion of this certificate by an authorized person shows that you have worked through all the parts of this workbook and satisfactorily completed the assessments. The certificate provides a record of what you have done that may be used for exemptions or as evidence of prior learning against other nationally certificated qualifications.

superseries

Organizing and Delegating

....

has satisfactorily completed this workbook

Name of signatory ....

Position ....

Signature ....

Date ....

Official stamp

Pergamon
Flexible
Learning

Fifth Edition

superseries

FIFTH EDITION

Workbooks in the series:

Achieving Objectives Through Time Management	978-0-08-046415-2
Building the Team	978-0-08-046412-1
Coaching and Training your Work Team	978-0-08-046418-3
Communicating One-to-One at Work	978-0-08-046438-1
Developing Yourself and Others	978-0-08-046414-5
Effective Meetings for Managers	978-0-08-046439-8
Giving Briefings and Making Presentations in the Workplace	978-0-08-046436-7
Influencing Others at Work	978-0-08-046435-0
Introduction to Leadership	978-0-08-046411-4
Managing Conflict in the Workplace	978-0-08-046416-9
Managing Creativity and Innovation in the Workplace	978-0-08-046441-1
Managing Customer Service	978-0-08-046419-0
Managing Health and Safety at Work	978-0-08-046426-8
Managing Performance	978-0-08-046429-9
Managing Projects	978-0-08-046425-1
Managing Stress in the Workplace	978-0-08-046417-6
Managing the Effective Use of Equipment	978-0-08-046432-9
Managing the Efficient Use of Materials	978-0-08-046431-2
Managing the Employment Relationship	978-0-08-046443-5
Marketing for Managers	978-0-08-046974-4
Motivating to Perform in the Workplace	978-0-08-046413-8
Obtaining Information for Effective Management	978-0-08-046434-3
Organizing and Delegating	978-0-08-046422-0
Planning Change in the Workplace	978-0-08-046444-2
Planning to Work Efficiently	978-0-08-046421-3
Providing Quality to Customers	978-0-08-046420-6
Recruiting, Selecting and Inducting New Staff in the Workplace	978-0-08-046442-8
Solving Problems and Making Decisions	978-0-08-046423-7
Understanding Change in the Workplace	978-0-08-046424-4
Understanding Culture and Ethics in Organizations	978-0-08-046428-2
Understanding Organizations in their Context	978-0-08-046427-5
Understanding the Communication Process in the Workplace	978-0-08-046433-6
Understanding Workplace Information Systems	978-0-08-046440-4
Working with Costs and Budgets	978-0-08-046430-5
Writing for Business	978-0-08-046437-4

For prices and availability please telephone our order helpline
or email

+44 (0) 1865 474010
directorders@elsevier.com